The Challenge to Change

The Challenge to Change
The Church Confronts the Future

by FRANÇOIS HOUTART

edited by Mary Anne Chouteau

SHEED AND WARD : : *New York*

Manufactured in the United States of America

Editor's Note

The material for this book was edited from a series of ten lectures given in August, 1963, by Abbé François Houtart, director of the Center for Socio-Religious Research, Brussels, Belgium. In editing these lectures I have tried to maintain, as much as possible, the vitality of the speaker-audience relationship.

The lectures formed a part of the fifth Marquette University Workshop in Curriculum and Role of the Faculty in the Formation of Sisters. They were sponsored by the Sister Formation Conference, Washington, D.C.*

Abbé Houtart's contribution to the workshop is of such scope and quality that the layman as well as the religious can benefit from the insight and understanding he brings to an examination of this world we all inhabit and to the mission in the Church we all share.

—MARY ANNE CHOUTEAU

Ash Wednesday, 1964

* The Sister Formation Conference is a section of the National Catholic Educational Association. Headquarters are at 1785 Massachusetts Avenue, N.W., Washington, D.C.

Author's Note

This was a very rapid and quite informal description of some of the questions put to the Church in a changing world. I am very well aware that the detailed complexities of these problems cannot be fully surveyed in these pages, but they can, perhaps, be put into a more realistic focus. The aim of this work is to help in the creation of a new spirit, a new dynamism, a new optimism among Christians in the present world.

The belief that the Holy Spirit actually works in the world is the basis for such an attitude. We don't disregard the many human failures, of course. We do not think, either, that facts are normative. But we do think that they offer us a means of discovering God's will and participating more fully in the Redemption.

May this work be a modest contribution to the great appeal made by Pope John's calling of the Council so that there would be a renewal in the Church and a new challenge for the world.

Contents

Contents

The Challenge to Change

Introduction

In order to speak precisely and relevantly about the mission of the Church in the world today, a world characterized by its dependence upon the developments and advances of technology, it is both useful and necessary to review briefly the sociological background from which Vatican II emerged. Much of what I intend to tell you will not be new to you. There will be many ideas with which you are, perhaps, already familiar. But I will try to bring together all that knowledge of the world today which you already have into some kind of global vision, a sort of world-wide synthesis which will help to bring us *to a better adaptation to this world where we must work.*

In our approach to a global vision we must strive to maintain an attitude that is threefold. First of all, we must approach the world in *spiritual terms,* with an attitude of fidelity to the Holy Spirit, an attitude of fidelity to the will of God for us, to help us to work along the line of the mission of the Church in the modern world. Even when we speak of a "sociological" approach, we refer to one that is directed by a spiritual attitude, by the fact that we believe God speaks to us, not only in the Gospel, not only through the tradition of the Church, but also in the facts, the conditions that exist in the world of today. This is a true spiritual attitude.

Second, we shall try to apply to this world we are seeking to envision, this Church in our technological society, a *sociological approach*. And when we use this term we do not use it in the sense of "social doctrine," but with the meaning which is given to it everywhere else, that is, a positive approach to social problems, a science of observation, and consequently, as such, neither profane nor sacred. It is in this sense that we shall try to approach reality, as something we *can* observe, something we can take hold of.

Third, we shall try to keep a *"prospective" attitude*. "Prospective" is a new word for a new science, a science of the future which, by assessing facts of the past and trends in the present, will try to predict future developments in man's situation. Some of the better-known examples of prospective are the demographic studies, evaluations of what the world's population will be ten or twenty years from now, based upon knowledge of the number of people in the world today, and taking into account the birth and death rates, and so on. This approach is being used more and more frequently, and while we shall not try to use the science of prospective in all that we shall try to see, we shall try, at least, to have a prospective mind. This will enable us to see the Church not only as it is today, but as it will be ten years from now, and twenty years from now, which we need to do, because we have to build the Church of tomorrow.

These three attitudes, then, we shall try to maintain throughout: the spiritual attitude as the point of departure, the sociological approach to the problem, and a prospective vision.

THE SOCIOLOGICAL BACKGROUND OF THE COUNCIL

We shall examine, then, the sociological background of the Council. This is not just a fine phrase, you know, but represents a profound reality. The Council had and has a sociological background; it did not just happen. Many realities in the world and in the Church together provided the circumstances which led to the convocation of Vatican II. The truly significant factor is that this Council was not called to combat heresy, as were the majority of the other councils, but has instead, from its very beginning, sounded a positive challenge to the Church to adapt herself to the new world, to the new circumstances of the life of mankind, in order to carry out in the most effective manner possible the mandate given by Jesus to "Go and teach the whole world."

This mission has taken on a profound significance in the world as we now know it. It is no longer a predominantly geographical problem because Christianity is present now in almost every country on earth. But we in the Church are, nonetheless, facing a new frontier, one that is not geographical but cultural and scientific. We are confronting a humanity which is rapidly becoming more and more master of the world with all kinds of breakthroughs in the fields of biology, psychology, and sociology, and in the discovery of new worlds. And if this is the world we are now facing, which the Church is facing, it is necessary that we be *aware* of this and that we learn more and more about all these fields.

We must, therefore, see the mission of the Church today in a real "world vision" because we are facing, actually, a "planetarization" of the world. The world is becoming a unity from the technological point of view, from the point of view of scientific discoveries, of geographical distance, of communications, and especially of telecommunication, which is only beginning.

We can no longer think of any kind of action, attitude, mission, congregation, institution, or of any Christian, except within the context of the universal situation of the Church in the world. The time of isolation is past. There are no longer private islands in the world or in the Church, either geographically or culturally. Every region in the world, every local church throughout the world, is now part of our ecumenical responsibility—which is to say that whatever we do anywhere can have and often does have immediate world repercussions. The attitude of some pastors in Colombia, South America, for example, towards the Protestants in Colombia (however understandable it might be in the Colombian situation) has, none the less, adverse world repercussions and intereferes with the progress of the ecumenical movement.

We may not, therefore, remain marginal, on the periphery of all that is happening, completely outside this world. For how can the modern world be attracted to Christianity, and this means Christ, if we stay outside the world or speak to it in terms of things which no longer exist? Or how can we Christians, without *knowing* the world of today, effect an incarnation of Christianity within this world? For we, as Christians, are called upon to be the light of the world today. To do less than this would be a real infidelity to the mission we have received from Christ.

This is one of the main problems of the Church today, as Pope John realized so well: that because of rapid technological developments we are really living in a new kind of civilization, an age of perpetual change, and the Church must discover the great characteristics of this new world in order to shed her light upon it.

PART ONE

Technical Civilization

"*Despite its defects and its mistakes, I love my age. I love its aspirations and its resolves. I revel in its feats of valor, its industries, and its discoveries. I thank it for its many benefactions to my fellow-men, for its warm affections proffered to the people rather than to prince and ruler. I seek no backward voyage across the sea of time; I will ever press forward. I believe that God intends the present to be better than the past and the future to be better than the present.*"

—ARCHBISHOP JOHN IRELAND

Probably the most significant single characteristic of the world today is that mankind is living in what we can speak of as a technical civilization, a civilization of man in conquest of nature, a conquest which he is advancing, using nature as a tool for progress—progress from the material, the cultural, and it may be also from the spiritual point of view. This last possibility has not always been recognized by the Church, which has all too often taken a critical and condemnatory attitude toward all progress in the world. Pope John, however, in his opening talk to the Council, took a most optimistic and positive view of the evolution of mankind and of technical progress. This view does not overlook the problems, but it certainly requires a new attitude regarding the present-day changes in the world on the part of many in the Church who have until now condemned this progressive change. It calls for our learning more about the realities involved before making moral judgments.

To assess the influences technical civilization has had on human lives, and thus on the work of the Church in the world today, it is necessary to consider the origin and development of this type of society.

1 *Origin and Consequences*

The technological age is often presented to us as belonging entirely to the material order, as though it had just come about by accident and was now overwhelming the spiritual side of man. But in fact technological civilization is first of all a *cultural* reality, not a material one. I am, of course, using the word "culture" in the sociological or anthropological sense, in which it means the whole of the values of a given society or group. It is in this sense that technological development is a manifestation of a cultural reality.

It is no accident that this type of civilization had its origin in the western world and not in India or Africa. The reason is that the culture of the western world, rooted in the Graeco-Roman tradition, had developed an attitude toward the world and nature which stressed the value of positive research. This has been especially true since the fifteenth century. Since then there has been emphasis not only on research as an approach to realities, but also upon experimental knowledge, which is the source of real science. The application of scientific discoveries to daily life, together with the value placed on research itself, has led to the development of a technical civilization. Of course other factors such as climate and geography have contributed.

Now I do not say that technical advancement is, in itself, either a good thing or a bad thing. Nor do I say, for example, that it is more valuable from an ultimate point of view for the Indian to cherish a philosophy which does not emphasize the worth of research but instead the worth of a mystical attitude to life. I do not say that one approach is better than another from the moral point of view. I simply make the observation that both approaches *exist*. These attitudes are facts, and we have no right to feel a sense of superiority over other countries whose cultures are underdeveloped from the technological point of view. And to consider cultures as "better" or "worse" from the standpoint of their technological development is to equate a sense of values with a moral judgment and this, in my view, means professional deformation: to pass moral judgment on everything, when what is called for is a sociological judgment, a matter of observation.

We must realize, however, that even though we are not deputed to bring it into being because of any inherent moral superiority, this type of civilization is now extending itself to the whole world owing to the consequences of technology. We are now witness to the encounter between technological civilization and the various traditional cultures in the world. This meeting has had many

results for the Church, both from the religious and the
pastoral points of view. As I review them, I am sure that
you will immediately see how they affect our work in the
world today.

CHANGES IN SOCIAL VALUES

The first great consequence of this encounter is a *change
in social values,* a change in the ideas, the concepts, the
things which have meaning for people. These values can
be very different from one culture to another. Why do
such changes occur? Because a technical civilization is
cultural in its origin and in its development and therefore
has very great and deep cultural consequences affecting
people's values and attitudes. To illustrate: one of the
determining characteristics of a culture is the attitude of a
man before the world, his vision of the world and of his
place in it. A technical civilization brings completely new
attitudes to a man's ideas of the world, of life, of time.
You can just imagine, for instance, the changes in attitude
that must take place in the "underdeveloped" countries
with the coming of technological advancement.

To begin with, most of these countries have a large rural
population whose ideas and attitudes regarding nature
and agriculture have resulted from all the centuries during
which these people and their ancestors have lived with
nature without understanding nature, without being its

master. And since they have been more or less at the mercy
of all the changes in nature, defenseless against the great
problems created by natural disasters, certain attitudes
and superstitions have developed in which religion has
played a sort of "biological" role: to defend man, his
health, his life, his crops against the ravages of nature.
This is why you have so often in rural populations in
Europe, and here too, I suppose, so many kinds of religious
gestures against illness, some of which are extraordinarily
mixed up with all kinds of superstitions. This sort of thing
is their whole attitude toward nature.

I remember once in Colombia, a peasant came to see
the priest of a neighboring parish and asked to have his
land blessed. "You know, Father," he said, "this year I
really hesitated very much, because I just didn't know
what to do—whether to ask you to bless my land or to get
some fertilizer." The priest asked him why he hadn't gone
to his own pastor and was told: "Well, last year I went to
him and he blessed my land, but it was awful. The result
was disastrous!"

There you are. You can already see the change in attitude: hesitating between the blessing or the fertilizer!

In many countries of Latin America an experiment is
now in progress. By means of "radio schools" educators
are undertaking the work not only of teaching people to
read and write, but also of attempting to effect a change
in their approach toward nature, toward agriculture,
toward hygiene. In other words there is an attempt to effect

a cultural transformation from pre-technical attitudes to the ideas of a technological society. Whether we are attempting to make this change too rapidly is a question which has been raised, but the fact remains that profound changes in attitude are occurring in the greater part of humanity which until now has not possessed this technological development, changes in attitude toward the world of nature, agriculture, health, and toward life itself.

Most of the people of Latin American countries have had an attitude of fatalism toward life and death, which developed, really, because they had so little control over such things. Infant mortality was 60–80%, life expectancy was about 25 to 30 years, and people came to regard life with indifference, as something which happened to them and which was to be endured. I was often struck by the apparent indifference of these people toward death—a dead man, a dead child, even the mother of a family. Apparent indifference, almost no sentiment. But this attitude of fatalism is changing with the coming of technical civilization because man is becoming more and more able to control nature.

Changing, too, are their attitudes to time. One of the most difficult things to adapt yourself to when you go to places like Africa or Latin America is the difference in the conception of time. Of course they are equally puzzled by our attitude to it. They think we are born with a watch inside us, because everything we do is calculated, is measured by time. Why? Because we are used to a technical civilization with timetables for trains, buses, planes, boats. If we are not on time we miss the boat! And so it is with our schools, our work, everything that is scheduled in a technological world where time is measured not only in minutes but also in money. In the non-technical or pre-technical society time does not have this value, so together with advanced methods we are bringing also changes in the very tempo of the lives of these peoples.

In addition to these changing attitudes toward nature, life, and time we are, as a consequence of the technical revolution, witnessing the passage in society from the sacred to the secular. I do not mean this as a religious judgment, but as a sociological observation. That is, those customs, those practices, those things that are held sacred, which cannot change or be touched in a given civilization or culture, are decreasing in number with the coming of technology. This is so because one of the most striking characteristics of the technical world is constant, continual change. And this is not easy to accept.

Of course this has some influence from the religious point of view because many things which we have held sacred from some kind of religious motivation are, in fact, only human, and perhaps we may reach the point in a technological and secular society where religious values will be much purer, much less implicated in the whole set of cultural values than before. Therefore you can see how necessary it is for us to adapt our own institutions to this changing world. You can see that many of the customs of our religious orders which were initiated by the founders, and remain sacred to this day, will perhaps have to be changed to meet the needs of the present. And in doing this, we would only be acting as the founders of our congregations would have acted were they beginning new orders today.

Emergent Values

All these changes in values attendant upon the advent of a technological civilization are modified by emerging values which are inherent in a culture fostered by technology. It is certain, for example, that in a technical civilization we are coming to a much more rational type of society, where *rationality* has a greater influence and where all that is irrational is less and less valuable in the organization of society and of modern life. And so we, who are educating the children and young people of today, must ourselves be attentive to these rational values in order to integrate effectively with a technological civilization.

This suggests, of course, some immediate applications to religious functions whose origins date back to a pre-technological age when time was of less importance. Maybe we are becoming too conscious of time, but consider, for example, the religious ceremonies accompanying the consecration of a church which take more than three hours. This was very typical in a pre-technical society, where the whole day was given over to the ceremonies, and so was a normal and acceptable way of passing time. But with the kind of work our bishops have today, it is really not rational. Other applications suggest themselves.

Values in the type of *leadership* demanded in a technological society differ greatly from those of a pre-technical civilization. Formerly the older people held the real leadership in the community because the greater value in the pre-technological civilization which is stable, which does not change very much, is tradition. And the people who were more able to hand down the tradition, who were sure of the tradition, were the older people with a longer experience of life. It was a life which did not change. But in the modern world, the leadership is no longer necessarily with the older people. In a technical world the leadership falls to the most able people in their field, and this ability is not equivalent with age.

It may seem cruel to say so, but it is true that in a technological society old people are put on old age pensions. Indeed, it is a direct consequence of technical civilization that people are living longer, and that we have many more old people than before. And perhaps it is natural that a change in attitude toward leadership by the elderly should have come about when medical technology intervened in the process of natural selection. In other words, those people who lived to seventy years of age or more a hundred years ago were the stronger ones, not only physically but probably also temperamentally, and therefore exerted tremendous influence. This is not always so today, and this explains in part the changed attitude toward them.

This fact of a much greater increase in the number of older people in a technical civilization also explains the new *organization* of society: the whole system of social security, old-age pensions, but additionally the fact that in almost all fields of work we have an age limit, and it may be that we must come to that in the Church, too. Some religious orders elect a general for life, but even here this lifetime role is usually reserved for the head of the order: it is not given to local superiors. But we do have this problem in the Church; it affects bishops, cardinals, and pastors. It will not be easy to solve, but it must be considered.

One of the greatest social problems in a technological civilization is that of giving a role to all of the people. This is a very real challenge and, I think, one of the responsibilities of the Church, because the Church must always be attentive to the human aspects of society as well as the supernatural if she is to realize fully her mission in the world. In the United States especially, many psychologists and sociologists have already devoted much thought and study to the problems of older people, to activities and interests which will enable the "senior citizen" to take a more active part in community life rather than to feel he is sitting around waiting to die. This is a field which should engage the efforts of the sisterhoods also.

Principal Value: Adaptation

We can see, therefore, that our technical civilization is the beginning of a perpetually changing world because the developments and applications of science are always growing. It is understandable, then, that perhaps the single most important value in a changing society is a capacity for *adaptation*, for individuals and for institutions.

An awareness of this fact is very important for the Church because the Church will be seen as something valuable in the world today if she accepts the possibility of adaptation, and the necessity for continual revision of her work and institutions. We cannot make one adaptation good for the next two or three hundred years!

I remember very well an experience I had not long ago in Poland. I had a meeting with a group of young Marxist intellectuals who were publishing a review, and we discussed the attitudes of Marxism and communism toward religion. These young people were Marxists, but they did not conform to the communist party line especially in philosophy, science, and religion. They explained to me the attitude of the communist government in Poland toward Catholicism. Basically, the government's whole policy was to make the Church a *museum*, a relic of the past which could not attract the younger generation, the people living in a vital, developing society. And the irony was that the integralist-conservative elements in the Church herself had contributed to the ease with which this policy accomplished its purpose. It had succeeded very well, so well in fact that the youth of the country had almost no interest at all in the Church.

Recently, however, I was talking with a member of the Polish parliament, and he told me that within the last few years, since the time of Pope John and the Council, the youth of Poland are beginning to take an interest in the Church again because they can see that something is happening, that the Church has not become too fossilized to change, to meet new situations, to adapt herself.

NEW RELATIONS BETWEEN MAN AND NATURE

If one of the great consequences of technical civilization has been a change in social values—in the ideas, the attitudes which are important and meaningful to people— this change has come about concurrently with the new relations between man and nature occasioned by technological progress. Now man is not only able to defend himself against the blind forces of nature, but is able more and more to direct the course of nature itself, to orientate it and use the natural good for himself, for his progress. And this discovery, this knowledge, this mastery of nature, has extended to more and more fields: to geography, where, with the exception of some areas at the poles, exploration of the earth's surface is nearly complete; to chemistry, to energical knowledge—the knowledge of the sources of energy in the world: electricity, oil, atomic energy and so on; to outer space, with all the possibilities which its exploration can bring to the future of mankind.

All this knowledge, of course, means that man is more and more able to get control of all these natural resources, to organize and use them in a rational way, and to go on to even greater development and progress in the use of nature. When we realize just how much progress has been made, say, within the last ten years, we see that we are just at the beginning of a deeper discovery of nature, of a deeper knowledge of nature, and that this knowledge is increasing day by day, not only in man's awareness of his discoveries but in his utilization of them, so that the words of Genesis are living truth: man *is* becoming more and more "the master of the earth."

But even more revolutionary than man's conquest of external, physical nature is his new control over human nature: man is becoming more and more master of his own life. We have perhaps not given much thought to this, it is still something new to us, but it is perhaps one of the most revolutionary aspects of the world today as a result of technological civilization. It is true in two spheres: the biological sphere and the psychological sphere.

Advances in biological science have been spectacular in the past few decades. The year 1965 will be the first International Biological Year, with biologists from all over the world coming together to share their findings and to establish and increase teamwork in research. Already the applications of biological sciences to medicine have brought humanity to double the life expectancy in just the last fifty years. We still have some countries where the life expectancy (the statistical calculation of the number of years you can expect to live when you are born) is less than thirty years. But in all the biologically developed countries, the life expectancy is now beyond seventy years of age as a result of the winning battle that is being waged against more and more diseases.

But this increase in life expectancy has not only resulted in the fact that we are living longer, it has also created the now-famous problem of the demographic explosion, or the population explosion. Somewhat paradoxically, the increase in population is not due to an increase in the birth rate of certain countries, for in almost all countries, with few exceptions, the birth rate is decreasing. It is due rather to the diminution of infant mortality and the fact that people are living longer. All advances notwithstanding, the law that everyone must die some day is still in effect, but during the time when you have a rapid decrease in the death rate without such a rapid decrease in the birth rate, there is a rapid increase in population!

In the underdeveloped countries until just a few years ago, the death rate was very nearly equal to the birth rate. But what is happening is that through the processes of hygiene and medicine brought by technical civilization, the death rate in these countries is decreasing to about 10 per thousand as compared to a birth rate of about 40 per thousand. And when you consider that the population as a whole is still a very young population (because until just a few years ago the life expectancy in these countries was about 30 years), the difference between the birth rate and the death rate will become of enormous weight before the normalization brought about by an older population can occur.

There are other factors which contribute to this increase in world population. Despite the fact that in the developed countries there is a slight decrease in the birth rate, this is more than offset by the repercussions of the technological advances introduced in the underdeveloped countries. Even though in these countries the birth rate itself is not increasing, there is a far greater percentage of the population coming to a reproductive age. Twenty years ago in the underdeveloped countries only 40–50% of the people lived to an age when they were able to have children, now 80% are reaching this age. So in one generation the multiplication of population is very rapid.

This situation is, of course, temporary, because it is

impossible that it should endure for long. Just to give one example of what I mean: The country of Jamaica now has 1.6 million inhabitants. With 3% increase of population a year, which is a high rate of increase but normal in all those countries now developing, within one hundred years there would be in Jamaica 29 million people, and at the same rate of increase in six hundred years there would be 50,000 billion people on this small island! Well this, you understand, although theoretically calculable, is just impossible.

But what is the meaning of this? This means that the limitation of the biological expansion of mankind is no longer a blind process but a rational one.

In all countries in the world and until just a few years ago in our own countries, mankind was limited by illnesses and by death, by the fact that 50–60% of the children were dying before the age of one year, by the fact that the average life span was 30–35 years, by the fact that married life was less fertile than now because of poor nutrition, and so on. But now we are living in an age when almost all children born in normal conditions are surviving; where married life is no longer of 10 or 20 years' duration but of 35, 40 or 50 years; where puberty is reached more rapidly among the youth, and the duration of the age of fertility is increasing. Consequently the potential biological expansion of mankind has increased tremendously.

Some attempt to limit population has always been in effect among mankind, however, because the number of people you can have on earth depends to a great extent on the possibilities which exist for feeding them. Because technology has developed more and better methods of agriculture we can, of course, support a much larger population than was possible two hundred years ago. But even in the Middle Ages some means were utilized to limit the population. The great numbers of people in convents and monasteries during the late Middle Ages were not all there as a result of supernatural religious vocations! Many were just sent there as a solution to a social problem. Another limiting factor on population increase, very well known and practiced in Ireland even today, was late marriage. In many peasant societies the families did not like to divide their land, and so the children had to wait until the father was too old, or died, to marry and take over the farm. Other means were, of course, utilized that were less humanitarian.

A consideration of these facts leads to two observations. First, that the progress in technology in the biological field has brought man to a completely new situation not only in face of nature, external physical nature, but with regard to his own existence. Second, that the limitation of mankind which was the normal thing, and which has always been in effect among all other living things as well, and has heretofore been influenced by ungovernable natural factors, is now, and will be more and more, in the hands of man himself.

These new situations not only present the problems of

birth control and other related moral issues, but also the more profound problem of the whole attitude of man toward his own life. We, as Catholics, must be careful not to approach these questions with what I might call a "morally simplistic" attitude. These are complex problems. Too often in the past our attitude has been so unqualified, so oversimplified, as to imply that people ought to have as large a family as is biologically possible; and this attitude is not only not rational, but I might even say not Christian in our present society, because biological conditions are now completely different, as well as social and economic conditions.

Taking into consideration all the biological changes which have resulted from technological development—the longer life-span, the low rate of infant mortality, the increase of fertility—it is not hard to see that having children in a technical, organized society is something very different from having children in the pre-technical rural society. In the rural, pre-technical society children who survived were economic capital because by the age of five or six they were capable of really contributing to the family economy. In our complex, technological society parents must provide their children with many years of education before they are sufficiently trained to make their own way, which means that children are dependent on their parents for many more years than was true in the pre-technical, rural society. And it is not only a question of the cost of education, but of the responsibility for preparing children to live in a complex civilization.

Once we have seen clearly the facts of such a new situation for man on earth, we must give a concrete ethical orientation. And this depends upon our conception of man. In the light of revelation we know that man is created superior to the other living creatures and cannot be treated like cattle. A lowering of the birth rate in the underdeveloped countries is not a matter of diffusing means of birth control and/or sterilization. It will be the result of a different approach to the facts of life, more rational—in other words, of a deep cultural change. And this does not happen all at once. Western civilization brought, along with the technical revolution, the demographic explosion. We have the responsibility of educating people to accept a "human" change of attitude, which will take time. This means also the duty of assisting economic development and cultural change.

For the technically developed regions, where, as we said, the meaning of the child has changed, and where the responsibilities of the parents have considerably increased, we don't have to conclude that a large family is no longer a value. But the large family today must be a responsible family, and this involves a conscious vocation for the parents. And surely this is a testimony of responsibility, confidence in God, and generosity.

When we discuss these human problems, then, it is

necessary to look at them in a global perspective—to see how the world has changed—before making moral judgments about them, because we can be so wrong if we judge everything in terms of another civilization, of another way of living for mankind. This is not only true in biology, it is also true in psychology.

Present-day progress in psychiatry and all the possibilities of its application are really extraordinary. Mankind is now in a position to gain new knowledge of all human reactions, of man's process of evolution, of his unconscious and subconscious worlds. But all these developments, you understand, have to be viewed in the framework of a new ethic. Because these are new problems, problems which have not existed before now, and consequently they have yet to be treated from the standpoint of ethics. And this is why the Church has such an important role in the life of mankind today. We have to bring to the people of all these countries new ethics for the rational process of demographic increase, the utilization of psychological research and psychiatric action, the utilization of the new psychological knowledge in the approach to the masses—for example in publicity, in political propaganda, in "brain-washing."

So the need for new ethics to deal with all these things results from scientific research and new discoveries which bring us as a consequence to a new kind of relationship between man and nature.

NEW SOCIAL RELATIONS

Technical civilization brings about not only changes in social values, not only new relationships between man and nature, but also changes in the relations between man and man in society, *new social relations.* It is not difficult to understand why, in such a process of change, the whole structure of society undergoes an almost complete reorganization. All the social relations among people are changing, the social institutions are changing, the types of communication between people are changing, the whole organization of economic life is completely changing.

This is not just a minor change, but, in a sense, a real mutation of mankind, and because we are just in the midst of it, it is so important that we become aware of what has happened and what is in the process of happening, for we are facing quite a few new kinds of phenomena which affect all the institutions of society, from the family, to the political, to the economic, even to the religious.

Specialization of Social Function

The first major change in the social relations of men which has come about as a result of technical civilization is the *specialization of social function.* What does this mean?

To put it as simply as possible: in every kind of society,

from the most primitive to the most elaborate, there have always been some answers to social needs. What are social needs? The basic social unit, of course, is the family, which is necessary for the continuation of the social group. We also need some process of socialization, some process of being introduced to the social values of the group, which means education. Any society needs some form of education. Any society needs also some form of organization, and this is political life. Any society needs to live, materially speaking, and this demands some form of economic life. Any society needs to have some leisure time. And in any society and in any human group we find some form of religious activities. All of these social needs are common human requirements and must be met in any and every type of human society. But the institutions performing the social functions necessary for family life, education, organized society, material support for man, leisure, and religion are very, very different.

In the pre-technical society it was very typical for all these social functions to be performed by one, or two, or three basic institutions.

Take, for example, the patriarchal type of family which is still prevalent in many parts of Africa, Latin America, and Asia. The patriarchal family not only performed the function of continuity in the group, which is directly the primary family function, it also fulfilled educational needs. And in great measure it satisfied the economic function because it served both as the unit of production and the unit of consumption. There was no problem of distribution except among members of the family. It was also the basic institution of what we could call political life and, together with the clan, formed to a great extent the recreational institution. In a rural, pre-technical society, the village performed practically all the social functions for the life of the people, and it was sufficient for them. And from the religious point of view the parish was the only religious institution and could respond to practically all the religious needs of the people.

It can be seen, therefore, that in a pre-technical civilization the typical social institution was a *polyvalent* institution, which means an institution which had *many* aims, values, and functions. But now in our technological society, because all these functions are becoming more specialized, we have a great number of *monovalent* institutions, that is, institutions with *one* aim, very definite and well-established. And this is true in all fields.

Let us consider, for example, the changes in the economic field. With the coming of technological development our economy has become more and more specialized. Whereas a relatively simple exchange economy existed in the pre-technical society, today, because of increased productivity brought about by technical possibilities, people cannot themselves consume all the goods they are able to produce, and so we have had for some time now a *market* economy. With the technological industrial revolution and the passage from a simple exchange or barter economy to a market economy, money was created as a tool to facilitate the exchange of merchandise. Increased production resulted in a whole new sector of economic life: *distribution,* carried on by a series of firms set up between producers and consumers. And today because production has become so specialized, because the market is flooded with so many products, and every day with new ones, another specialized segment of economic life has come into existence: *publicity,* which informs the public about all these products. We could go on and on.

It is not necessary to go into detail about all the specific functions performed within each of these major sectors in the economic field to realize just how complex and specialized economic life has become.

Or consider the changes in education. Until just a few decades ago, a grammar school education met the needs of all but a few members of society. But now, with the necessity for preparing children and young men and women to take their place in a highly specialized and complex society, their educational needs have become correspondingly specialized and complex. What was formerly capable of being performed by a single institution is now carried on by a multiplicity of specialized institutions, ranging from vocational, technical institutions to the universities with all their fields of specialization.

The needs of leisure, too, are undertaken by a great many institutions: organized sports, clubs, scouting, and so on.

What is really characteristic, then, of all technical
civilizations is the fact that all these social functions are
performed by more and more monovalent types of institutions, and that there is an increasing number of institutions
at the disposal of human beings who live in this type of
society. This increasing number of specialized institutions
for the economy, for social organization, for education, for
leisure—indeed, for all kinds of human activities—is a very
important factor because it creates a completely new kind
of life among men and is the underlying reason for the
type of urbanization we now have.

Urbanization as we know it now has been the result of
the specialization of social functions. The new dimensions
produced by the increase of complementary forms of
industrial activities required that more and more people
be brought together to perform these specialized functions. This resulted in a new, specialized land use in cities:
business centers, administrative buildings, schools, parks,
stadiums, concentrations of industry, and also some
localization of the different social classes. So that when
we think of the organization of a social or cultural apostolate in a city, it has become impossible to see the city as
just a sum of neighborhoods; it must be seen as a complex
whole of the specialized functions which are performed in
it. If one family is living near a large school or another in
an industrialized neighborhood, it is not especially because
these activities are a part of this or that family's life, but
because they are a part of the city's life. And the fact that

all the many social needs of the community are being met in different sections of the city is bringing about new types of social relations among people.

When people were meeting each other continually in the polyvalent institutions of the patriarchal family, the small village or the rural parish, they came to know each other very well. They had what are called in psychology or sociology "primary" types of relations with each other, which means a face-to-face knowing of each other from almost all the aspects of personality. This type of relationship still exists in the city, of course, but a new type of social relationship has greatly increased in city life. This is the "secondary" type of social relationship, which means, briefly, that when we live in a city we meet quite a number of people just because we are engaging in quite a few social activities: we go to the office, to the movies, to the supermarket, to the drugstore, to the department store; we take the bus, the train, and so on. So these activities involve a new type of social relationship which is very slight and limited to the service side of social relations that form a great part of life in a technological civilization.

For example, we may know a man because he is a teller at a bank, but we don't know who his wife is or whether he has children; or, if so, whether they are attending public or Catholic schools; whether he is a Democrat or a Republican; whether he reads Shakespeare or Spillane. We know him because he is performing a service, and he does not expect us to be his close friends just because we deal with the bank at which he works. We may, of course, become friends, but it is just impossible to know personally and intimately all the people with whom we come into contact so briefly. We would really go out of our minds if we were to attempt such a thing.

We need not think that the secondary type of relations between people is morally less good than the primary type of relation. Again we must avoid making a moral evaluation in our apostolic work before understanding how things have necessarily changed in a technical and urban civilization. We must also develop a Christian way of engaging in secondary types of relationships, which is quite possible and quite necessary, but which does not involve immediately changing the relationship to one of the primary type.

Mobility

Another factor which contributes to the new social relations among men in a technological society and is closely related to the development of specialized social functions in urban life is the *mobility* of the population.

When we analyze the life of today, it is increasingly evident that we have become a mobile society, with a very high percentage of people moving from one house to another, from one neighborhood to another, from one city to another. The degree of mobility is even greater in the United States than in Europe because the simpler taxation system here makes it easier to buy and sell homes.

But even in Europe, in, say, the city of Brussels, which has a million inhabitants, in ten years 1,750,000 people have moved. Statistically speaking, this means that almost everyone has moved twice in ten years. Or take a small city in Belgium where 100 new houses were built. By the time these houses were occupied 800 moves had occurred, because a family moved into the home left unoccupied by the family who moved into the new house, and so on down the line. And this is happening all the time in cities because of increased population and because we are no longer building for 500 years; there is constant need for new building, and wherever the building industry flourishes it is a sign that the population is mobile.

Not only do people move frequently from one house to another, they commute daily from home to city, and especially from suburban homes to the city streets. Take, for example, these figures concerning the city of Chicago ten years ago: some five thousand people there at night, who had their homes on streets in the "Loop"; but during the day these same streets held a population of 900,000 people! There is moreover a week-end or vacation mobility which is now tremendous. All over, not only here in the United States but also increasingly in Europe, we have become a "car civilization." For example, two years ago in Paris it was estimated that more than 2,000,000 people left Paris for the day of Pentecost. And during the two months of July and August the tourist population in France alone was 23,000,000 people. It is estimated that now 60% of the people in England are vacationing elsewhere than the home in which they spend the winter.

The necessity for daily mobility, then, is the result of this specialization of social function because the monovalent institutions which have developed for work, for leisure, for school, for living are all located in different places. So the mobility of the population of the technically developed societies is ever-increasing and carries with it the increasing problem of the organization of circulation both within the city and throughout the country.

All institutions are affected by this mobility: educational, political, economic, but especially religious institutions. Think, for example, of the parish. What is happening to parish life is happening because of the mobility of the people. One French layman put it this way. "Well, you see, *before* the pastor was saying 'My parishioners' and *now* the parishioners are saying 'My pastors.'" This is a result of moving from one parish to another in the city, moving during week-ends, moving during vacations. In our cities more and more of the parish churches are nearly empty on the great liturgical feasts, like Easter or Pentecost. So you see how this affects us and why we must rethink many aspects of our religious parish life in the light of these social facts.

A recognition of how the parochial relationship has

changed and continues to change is very important because we are still thinking in very old concepts, I would say, especially in our Catholic world when we talk about the integration of man, of people, of what a good Christian family is. What we are saying very often is that for us a good Christian family (at least in Europe) is an immobile family, which goes to Mass every Sunday in the parish church and which does not move away because it has to be known by the pastor. So we have a concept of the integrated man which is still modeled on the old type of society, whereas the truly integrated man in modern city life is highly mobile. The integration of man in a modern urbanized technical society is really determined by his capacity for mobility, because when a man has no possibility of moving, of choosing his work, his leisure, his education, he must remain on the margin of society.

The whole problem of mobility brings us to the importance and relevance of the liturgical movement today. Because, owing to this factor, the community of worshippers in our churches will be less and less a natural geographical one; people must be integrated from the religious point of view: by religious values and by religious practice. We have to build the integration of Christian life, Christian community, not on the basis of some geographical concept—on a territorial parish with all the people living in that territory knowing each other and making a community—not on this geographical concept, but on the fundamental value of the Eucharistic community.

We simply must face the fact that the small parish of 500 or 1,000 people, small enough for the pastor to have some opportunity of knowing each family personally, is fast disappearing, and that even a great part of the parochial renewal in Europe is based on a false sociological premise: that it will be possible to make a "village in the city" and bring together all the people of the city parish into the social relationships of village life. This simply cannot be done, except for a very small part of the population. So we must increase our efforts toward the integration of the Christian community by building up a community around the Eucharistic function, around the actualization, the realization, of Eucharistic community. This means that all the people coming to Mass in any parish church will feel a sense of community, not only spiritually, not only supernaturally, but also psychologically and sociologically.

That is why the liturgical movement is so very important in our technological society: it gives us the means to create a community around the altar. That is why it is so important to have a real participation of the people in the Mass, to have a renewal of church architecture; why, for example, in almost all the new churches in Germany, France, Belgium, Holland, Switzerland, and here, too, in the United States, we put the altar in the center of the church and the people around it; why the Mass is more and more being said facing the people; why we have the community answering the Mass, singing the Mass; why we have sought the use of the vernacular languages: all these are means of bringing people to a sense of real community around the altar. And this sense of Eucharistic community which is established around the altar, which is actualized in the Mass, in the Eucharistic sacrifice, should lead to an ever greater sense of the community of all Christians in the Mystical Body of Christ.

So the unity of the small rural parish which is broken up by the consequences of an urban, mobile society can be replaced with a more truly religious unity which knows no boundaries but can embrace the whole world.

Socialization

A third development in man's new relations with his fellow men is *socialization,* which means that as a result of technical civilization we have come to a way of life in which the collective form of existence is becoming more and more important. We must be prudent in not condemning socialization because it seems so near to socialism or communism; we must first understand the true meaning of socialization before making a moral evaluation. And the first thing we must understand about socialization is that *it is a social fact.* It is a social fact, very well defined in *Mater et Magistra,* that we are living in a more collective form of existence. This, as I observed before, is another consequence of the increasing development of technological society, which has contributed to the socialization of life in three ways.

First, the *specialization of social function,* which we have already considered to some extent. The fact that we no longer have one, or two, or three polyvalent institutions like the family, the small village, or the parish performing all the social functions, but that instead we have ever greater numbers of more and more specialized institutions for the economy, education, leisure, politics, and religion. This means that all social functions in a technological society are *interdependent.* We are not performing one function in one monovalent type of institution just for the people involved in that institution. We are not making shoes, for example, just for the people working in the shoe factories.

So there is really an interdependence of all social functions, not only economic, but also educational, recreational, political, religious. And because this interdependence is increasing, it is always a more complex type of interdependence which must be organized. This is what socialization means. We require a more collective form of economy, of political life, of leisure, of education because of the multiplicity of specialized institutions. This need not mean a complete usurpation of all individuality, a complete negation of personality, although this may be one of the dangers of the time in which we are living. Actually, however, in our modern society, to promote the welfare of the human individual, we must have some form

of socialization. This fact was very clearly perceived in
Mater et Magistra.

This interdependence of social functions is not just a
fact of any given society but is true of global society as
well. If we examine global society, we must come to the
conclusion that there is also more and more interdependence among nations. For example, just in looking over the
things we use every day, we find that a great many of them
come to us from all over the world. This is just a sign of
more and more interdependence because of specialization.
We shall examine the international organization in
political life later.

The second factor which has contributed to the socialization of life is *increased dimension* or scope, an ever-
widening range of influence in almost all fields.

New dimensions of production, for example, are responsible for a complete revolution in European economic
life, because Europe is obliged to form industrial com-
plexes rather than small, isolated types of industry. There
is a whole process of unification in our economy, in the
political sphere, because of the reality of new dimensions
in productivity. The same thing is true not only of the
industrial world, but also in agriculture.

But of course, because of these new dimensions we
must move toward more *organization,* and on a new level,
not merely national but international. Because we are
more and more dependent on each other, we are also more
and more involved in developing types of organization

where the social aspects of reality are increasingly important and where the powers of decision are more and more in the hands of collective organizations. This is a necessity, and not the proof of a communist ideology.

In production we are coming to new dimensions and new types of organization because of automation, the so-called second industrial revolution. We are faced with new dimensions in the field of scientific research. When we see what the needs for research in space are, for example, and how quickly this whole field is developing, we may be able to come much more easily and rapidly to some kind of agreement between Russia and the western countries because of the necessity for coming together to share the expense of space research. We need to have a greater world market to make the best use of productive processes. This need was behind the formation of the European Common Market, but even this market will have to be expanded.

So an increase in new dimensions is an underlying factor in socialization.

The third element in the socialization process is the increase of *communication*. The new types of communication we have developed, which contain such immense possibilities for increased contacts and reciprocal influences between men and nations and which must themselves be organized, have increased our interdependence. For example, the cost of developing the new super-jet that will make the trip between Europe and America in two and a half hours is so vast that it will have to be shared. The developments in telecommunications even within the last few months are such that before long we shall have our pick of the television programs in practically any country of the world, but it is not difficult to imagine the degree of organization that will be needed before the full possibilities are realized. We in America are already accustomed to dialing any city in the nation just from the telephone on our desk, and now it is about the same in Europe.

But all these developments in our social life are the results of technology. The applications of techniques, of scientific discoveries, to our daily life are producing greater specialization, new dimensions, new communications. So we are really bringing about the necessity for socialization, or, in other words, the necessity of a better *organization* of society and the development of good moral, collective norms of living.

The collective objectives of mankind are becoming more and more numerous, and some of them are very urgent; for example, the problem of disarmament, space research, the development of the peaceful use of atomic energy; or the most pressing problem of all, underdevelopment. These problems are of such magnitude that they can be solved only if all the countries of the world can come together and join their resources.

So collective objectives call for collective means for their accomplishment. And the fact is that socialization is becoming a universal condition. We cannot think of any single type of society, even that of the United States, which will, or can, avoid socialization—any society in which a typical liberalistic, capitalistic, individualistic way of life could just go on. Even from the political and economic point of view, the United States is one of the most socialized countries in fact if not always in theory. But this socialization is normal; it could not be otherwise, and we must realize this so that we shall not attempt to develop values which cannot function in a socialized type of civilization and neglect values which are essential and relevant to the world in which we do live.

The consequences of this socialization are varied. I will mention just a few of them.

The first consequence is that we are facing a new kind of responsibility. We now have more and more *collective responsibilities,* and it is very difficult to adapt ourselves to this. It will take time, perhaps generations, for men to develop a real sense of responsibility in these new spheres —the economy, political life, education, and so on.

This is the main task of the laity because they are in the world. Of course they need the assistance of the clergy in the theological approach to these problems. It calls for teamwork, but it is not so much a question of laymen helping the clergy in the performance of their tasks as of the clergy helping the lay people.

Another consequence is that the *intervention of the state* is increasing. Not the state in the medieval concept of the prince, or even in the "liberal" concept of a public organization which exists to look on, and eventually to intervene when abuses in the exercise of a free-enterprise system become too great, but the state conceived as a collective organization of all the people, not just the few, which can take the initiative in the organization of the economy. This concept of the state is much more apparent in the developing countries, where a planned process of development is vitally necessary. But even in the developed countries the state has more power than before to regulate social conflicts, to regulate traffic, to regulate the rate of bank interest. And the power of the state to influence the economy indirectly—as, for example, the economic impact of the military defense budget, research, and development on many of our countries—is tremendous.

A final consequence of socialization, though by no means the last in importance, is that nowadays in almost all fields *teamwork* is absolutely necessary to accomplish anything.

We can see, too, some consequences for the Church. I have said that we are living in a world of new frontiers for the Church; socialization presents us with a new frontier. We are challenged specifically to explore and develop two problem areas.

The first is the challenge to break up what I would call our *parochialism*—not our parishes, do not misunderstand me—but our parochialism. It is very strange, indeed something of a paradox, to see how in the Church—the very Church which has the most universal type of organization, which is the most international—there has developed among Catholics, and especially among priests and Sisters, this self-centered spirit of parochialism and congregationalism. This would be truly inexplicable unless we realized that most of our religious orders were formed in a polyvalent type of society, and were therefore concerned with and formed by the needs of pre-technical civilization.

Today, however, it is amazing, one might almost say appalling, to see the extent to which we are still oblivious to the rest of the world around us, how our only concern is our own small world, how in urban pastoral work we are still basically oriented to a rural parochial system, despite the vast changes which have taken place in our society.

The Church must, therefore, break the confining bonds of this parochialism and religious congregationalism because we can no longer solve our present problems in isolation from each other, within each parish or each religious order. We must work for the increase of interparochialism and inter-congregationalism, not only in spirit but in action. The fact that so many different religious orders are present at the Sister Formation Workshops is already positive evidence that progress is being made. But we must go much further. We must actually *organize* in the Church many more inter-congregational types of institutions and practices, because this spirit of parochialism in the Church is one of the major obstacles to her universality. And we are living in a really blessed time to promote the universality of the Church.

The second great challenge to the Church as a result of socialization is for the *creation of a system of moral values* for living in a socialized society. "Creation" is perhaps too strong a word because it might seem to imply that we have nothing, and we already have, of course, a great deal. But we must develop what we already have, expand it as our world has expanded, and apply these moral principles to the world as it exists today. We have greater collective responsibilities now than ever before, and we must learn to accept them. The two encyclicals, *Mater et Magistra* and *Pacem in Terris,* have given a very clear orientation on moral values for our present world situation, but we must continue to study world conditions and be ready to meet new challenges with relevant responses. As a theologian said one day: "We don't have to follow the encyclicals, we have to precede them!" I don't think we shall have to wait thirty years anymore for an encyclical on moral social values; we need one, at least one, every five years.

It will be necessary also in the college and novitiate curricula to be more attentive to a consideration of moral values which are relevant to contemporary society. This will require very well-trained theologians, not just people commenting on treatises in scholastic theology which has been the same since St. Thomas. I do not say that the moral theology of St. Thomas is completely obsolete, you understand, but a few things have happened in the last seven hundred years! So just to discuss a classical treatise —well, this is easy in a way; you don't need very well-formed theologians. But to be able to give insights into contemporary problems in a way that is related to one's spiritual and apostolic life, to distinguish between what is certain and never changing and what is still a matter of research and hypothesis among theologians, is much more difficult. For this we need very well-trained theologians, and we shall not have a thousand of them. So again the need for some *organized* form of co-operation among priests, religious orders, and laymen.

We need courses also in what I would call the *sociological approach* to the world and to the role of the Church in the world because formation along this line is necessary, really, for all of us: priests, Sisters, and Christian laymen. We must provide the opportunity for the formation of minds able to understand and distinguish the problems of world society and to relate the role of the Church acting in this society, in a positive way, with positive scientific approaches to actual existing world conditions. It will not, perhaps, be necessary to add more sociology courses to the curriculum, but only to re-orient some of the existing courses in sociology and to present these under the best teachers.

Again, highly trained specialists in this field, as in the field of theology, do not number in the thousands. So here,

too, there is need for new organization among our educational institutions in order to provide the best training
available. For example, if we could have for the whole
country some Sisters, or priests, or laymen formed along
these lines, with each one giving month-long, intensive
sessions in the regularly-scheduled courses in different
colleges, it would be possible to reach all the colleges
during a two-year cycle.

Such an effort, however, could succeed only with real
co-operation, with a real effort to eliminate the difficulties
and discords of parochialism and congregationalism, with
all those involved united by the same spiritual attitude of
fidelity to the will of God in carrying out the mission of
the Church according to the needs of the present world.

Communication

Our new relations between man and man, the new social
relations, have been influenced not only by the specialization of social functions, by mobility, by socialization, but
also by new dimensions in *communication.*

We have already discussed at some length the *geographical* dimensions of communication: mobility, jet trans-
portation, telecommunication, which have increased to
such an extent that the community which is centered only
on a local geographical type of relationship is living a
marginal life in a technological civilization.

When we consider that the Church has organized her pastoral life almost wholly on the basis of a territorial parish, we can see the danger to her missionary influence in the world in having become too much identified with small local communities. This is true even in the United States, although the parish system here is far better than in most countries of Europe. In the United States some kind of geographical community has been conserved in American urban life, and especially in suburban life, which is not the case in many European cities. In the United States there is also the fact that most of the clergy has been concentrated in urban parish work and consequently there is not the same problem as in Europe, which has a dispersion of very small rural parishes, so that, for example in France, only 7,000 priests serve nearly 25 million people in the big cities while about 49,000 priests are serving rural areas with a population of less than 20 million people! The same disproportion exists in Italy, in Spain, in Belgium. Even though there has been some improvement in the European city parishes in the last twenty years we still have parishes of as many as thirty thousand souls.

In the American cities, then, we have more parishes. This is, of course, much better for the parish type of apostolate. But the identity of the Church has, perhaps, become too closely bound up with the local geographical community. The accent on the local community makes the Church marginal to our present society and is indirectly responsible for the secularization of economic, political, and social life. The preoccupations of the clergy are too often only with the development of parish life, which is socially a world of children, of non-working women and of men at leisure. All the sectors of decision-making in society are outside the parochial concern of the clergy, and their view on the role of the layman in the apostolate is generally concentrated on what lay people may do to help the clergy in parochial activities.

All these situations have real implications which will affect our pastoral activities and will require that we make meaningful adaptations in order to give our people a spiritual formation, a wider vision of the world, and a total vision of life which is more truly Christian.

But not only have the geographical dimensions of the world changed from the small local community to include countries of the whole world because of the new developments in communication, the *ideological* dimensions of the world are also completely new as a consequence of increased communication. Now, as never before, people have a better knowledge of what is happening all over the world.

Now because of the press, radio, and television, people have more and more opportunities for making judgments on world events, for judging their own lives, their own actions, their own social institutions in comparison with others'. Now, as a result of new communication, we are, all of us, living in a pluralistic world. Even the smallest village in Latin America is no longer isolated from the ideological point of view.

I remember one Sunday after Mass in a small Indian village of the Cordillera. In the village square a blind Indian was reciting some poetry, a few verses, to try to make a little money. So I went to hear what he was saying. Well, he was making up a ballad about Caryl Chessman, the man who was executed in California a few years ago. And he was presenting Chessman as the victim of American capitalism. This was in a small Indian village in the mountains of South America. Why? Because of communication. I don't say he had all the facts straight, but there had been communication!

From the ideological point of view, then, we can say that we are living in a pluralistic society, and this type of society will most probably endure till the end of the world. It is not necessary to convince you of this, because here in the United States you have been conscious for a long time that you are living in a pluralistic society, composed of a mixture of ideologies, of religions, yet living together in the same communities, sharing together the same social life and the same social institutions. But those countries which think theirs is a Christian society because most of their people are still baptized in the Church are deluding themselves, for even they are living in a pluralistic world as a result of the ideological dimensions of communication, and they must become more aware of this fact.

Just one example. One day, by chance, I was watching

television in Belgium. As you perhaps know, sometimes all the European countries link up their television networks and have programs on "Eurovision." Well, this day on Eurovision we could watch the consecration of an Anglican bishop. This ceremony was shown all over Europe, and it was really very impressive. And you can see how witnessing this consecration would have had an impact, for example, on a Catholic population, just seeing that almost all the rites were exactly the same as the Catholic rites—the bishop in a miter, a Mass that was practically the same as the one in the Catholic Church—but all in English. Just to see that it was possible, that it was a lovely ceremony with beautiful singing, very close to Gregorian chant but all in English, not one world of Latin —this kind of thing really brings quite a few thoughts to the minds of Catholics, with regard to the use of Latin in the Church for instance.

So all of us must face the fact that we are living in a pluralistic world, and this will require adaptation in the Church to act in a pluralistic society from the ideological point of view. This is why we cannot remain marginal to the modern world, why we cannot become too much identified with social communities which are really typical of another age. I don't say that we must abandon work in local communities, because local communities still exist, but these are not the only type of social relations which must concern us. We must learn to look at life in its proper perspective, and today this requires a global vision.

I have said that especially in the cities of Europe the development of urban life differed from urban life in the United States in that the center of local community disappeared much more rapidly. But even so, when we consider the possible sphere of activity for all the priests in these cities, we see that most of them are completely identified with a local territory. They live there, their house is there, they work there. Their whole preoccupation is there. They adjust to one thing, the small territory in which they work, and lose little by little all concern for the other problems of life. This is why they appear so marginal, so far removed from the problems which concern modern man. And I believe this situation in Europe has had a real bearing on the decrease in vocations for the diocesan clergy: they seem like people living in another age.

But this is true also from the ideological point of view. How marginal we can appear in our small ghetto, in our refusal to participate with other people in other institutions. This exclusivism is still growing in some countries, this idea of increasing the number of things which are Catholic and only for Catholics. I can speak about this from experience because it is a situation which is developing in Belgium and has already reached a high degree of development in Holland, where, for example, almost the whole of life is organized for Catholics, or for Protestants or for Humanists—those who are neither Catholic nor Protestant. Not only the schools, but political life, the trade unions, the newspapers, the drugstores, everything.

Of course the financial burdens of the educational system, for example, are not a problem for Catholics because the state supervises and supports the educational systems of Catholics, Protestants, and Humanists. This has worked very efficiently, so that Catholic education has been able to expand without difficulty and to achieve a high degree of excellence. But a short time ago I was talking with the secretary of the Catholic schools in Holland and he told me that they are now beginning to wonder if this is really such an ideal situation. As things are now, he said, they have created a society of Catholics in Holland which is almost completely isolated from the rest of the people because they have their own institutions for everything. This has, in effect, created a type of pluralism so organized that the different groups seem almost to be living in different worlds rather than in an integrated society.

The most progressive thinkers among both Catholics and Protestants in Holland are coming to the conclusion that they went much too far in organizing this whole system, and they are now trying to find ways of bridging the gaps which divide the population. They have not yet agreed upon any solutions, but at least they can see that there is a problem.

The possibility of Catholic universities or colleges working together with state universities or non-Catholic universities in the very specialized fields of technical education is being considered, and this might be one way of coming together and of renewing communications with each other.

A special issue of *Social Compass,* the international review of socio-religious research, published some months ago, contained studies of religious pluralism in Germany, the United States, and the countries of Latin America. So, as I said, while we are not yet sure of the solutions, we are aware that the problem exists and will require attention.

International Organizations

The development of international life, of *international organization,* is another aspect of the new relations between man and man which exist as a consequence of technological civilization. Within the last thirty years we have seen the growth of many inter-governmental organizations. On a world basis we have the United Nations with all its specialized agencies, but organization has also developed on a regional basis.

In three years, more than thirty new countries have entered the United Nations. We have seen the development of the specialized agencies working in the UN: the Food and Agricultural Organization; UNESCO, the organization for culture and education; the World Organization for Health; the International Labor Organization, and all those other organizations which are called specialized because they have been established for special co-operation. These organizations are performing important functions, and it may be that they will have to come in the future to more executive functions, to more power of decision in the carrying out of their work. This is what Pope John XXIII envisioned in *Pacem in Terris* when he spoke of a new concept of world organization, of world government.

From the political international point of view we have experienced a great change in the attainment of independence, the decolonization, of more than one billion people since World War II, resulting in the birth of new nations and increasing the number of nations in the UN. This process of decolonization has been especially marked by a rise of national consciousness which has resulted from the rapidity of communication, so much so that, we have been told, the actual process of decolonization is going much more slowly than the formal process or even the political process in some respects. But decolonization, slow or rapid, is part of the march of progress and is impossible to stop. It must, however, result in organization.

Regional as well as international organizations are playing a very important role. There are, of course, regional organizations in the UN, such as the Council for Economic Development of Latin America and similar councils for Asia, Africa, and Europe, but those are dependent organizations of the UN. There are also other

regional organizations such as the seventy-five-year-old
Pan-American Union, one of the first of such organizations;
the Organization of American States; the European Economic Community, with different agencies like the Common Market and the Community of Coal and Steel; the
neutralist Casablanca group; and the movements toward
the orderly grouping of the African countries, such as the
Addis Ababa group, PAFMECSA.

And finally we have the development of private international organizations, which is something really phenomenal. There is even an International Yearbook with
the names of the international organizations of all types,
from scientific to business, from movies to international
laundry organizations.

All these organizations have developed as the logical
consequence of the new social relations among men
brought about by the birth and development of technical
civilization.

NEW EMPIRICAL BASIS FOR METAPHYSICS

The changes in the whole organization of human life,
the changes brought by the application of science and
technology, the changes in the relations between man and
nature, both biological and psychological: all these are
contributing to a new empirical basis for metaphysics.

Through all these technological discoveries and technical applications of the discoveries of science we are coming to a new anthropology and a new vision of the life of mankind. And this is very important.

First, the new anthropology. I do not have the competence to go into the scientific side of this very deeply, but in the new anthropological vision of man, he is seen not as an essentially spiritual being living in a material world with all the obstacles of the material element, but as a real *unity* of spirit and matter. Not as a spirit limited by matter, but just as a unity of human nature, where spirit is limited and matter is limited because man is a limited being. He is seen as a whole, a union of spirit and matter, in which the development of human nature is directed not only to the spiritual but also to the material, and human nature as a whole is viewed in its *unity* and not so much as *separated* into spirit and matter.

This new kind of vision of man is being amplified more and more by new discoveries in biology, where we find spirit so incarnated in matter, and so conditioned by matter, that we can no longer suppose we have a true vision of man if we make a division between them.

One of the most amazing new discoveries in biology is the fact that in all molecules and in all the smallest elements of life there is an incarnation of spirit, that each molecule, each atom of living matter, has its own code, somewhat like an IBM card, and that is why, for example, all the parts of the body develop themselves in a certain way. And that, furthermore, if we could change this code, the same molecules would produce something completely different, so that each small particle of matter is already an "incarnation" of some spirit, leading it to its own particular good. There is, in fact, so much spirit in all that is material, especially in human beings, that we now have a new view of what it is that preserves unity in creation.

This is, of course, from the natural point of view. From the Christian point of view, all this is really leading to a new vision of the reintegration of all things in Christ. We are being made more able to understand theology by the whole discovery of what nature is, and what man is. We can say, therefore, that with all these technological developments we are really building a new empirical basis for metaphysics, a new way of looking at the causes and character of nature and man. It is based upon actual, practical, proven experience and discoveries and is contributing to a new vision of the evolution of mankind. This new vision, starting from biological discoveries, brings us to the theory that there is an evolution in the whole of nature toward greater specialization and spiritualization.

This new vision of man is not only physical. It is also social. The fact that the world is coming to a closer unity is very evident, or at least the fact that technology is bringing us to a possibility of greater unity. This is why one of the great roles of the Church today is to build up, to develop, moral values for life in a more socialized world, a more unified world.

And so we come to the idea of Father Teilhard de Chardin, that all this progress is conducting mankind to what he calls the "Omega Point," so that the whole process is toward unity in God. This theory has not yet perhaps been completely formulated, but it has a strong appeal for non-Christians, because it is a real effort to integrate the whole knowledge of man and nature, and the whole new knowledge of the socialization of man, and the social evolution of mankind, into a spiritual vision, leading to the spiritualization of man and to unity in God. This development is not seen simply as a natural process, excluding the role of Redemption in the whole history of the world; rather it shows how man is guided by God toward his end. All the revolutionary facts about physical reality as something not static but dynamic, in perpetual change, which were first considered by Einstein, have a bearing on this view.

This revolution in a scientific approach to nature and to the whole natural world is very new and is really bringing about a renewal in some fields in the philosophical conception of nature, of time, and of quite a few other aspects of philosophy. The fact that the term "metaphysics" has fallen, to a great extent, into disuse is understandable, because this word conveys the idea of a cleavage between physics and metaphysics, and in this new vision of the world, philosophers are striving to explain the *unity* between the physical sphere and the sphere of thought.

Even if we are just at the beginning of this new

anthropological vision and of a new political vision, we are progressing more and more along these lines because we really are discovering a new world.

This is true, also, of ideology in the world—ideology in the sense of theory functioning as the intellectual pattern for practice—for concrete applications in human life. We have now, and perhaps shall always continue to have in the future, new kinds of ideologies which represent our attempt to bring together all the facts, all the new situations of man in the world, in order to create a new kind of action by man in the world.

One of the ideologies we have now is Marxism, which had its origin in the nineteenth century, but which is still functional, especially in the underdeveloped countries, because it offers an explanation of the origin of man, of his development, of the changes in the whole organization of society, with ideological assent to the changes as part of the mechanism which would bring mankind to a higher stage of development.

The great weakness of ideologies like Marxism, however, is that they have had their origin at specific moments in the evolution of mankind and are built up completely on the stage of knowledge people had reached at those particular times. And because of this fixed vision and the demand for rigid adherence to the party line, we now see the process of disintegration taking place. Marxist philosophers, scientists, and physicists are beginning to question whether the doctrine of dialectical materialism can accommodate itself to the discoveries of modern science which throw into discredit some of the basic tenets of the official materialistic philosophy of the party.

This is why, in the process of incarnating Christianity in the world, we must take care not to lose the transcendental character of Christianity, which enables it to adapt itself to any kind of change in civilization, in social organization, in philosophy—to any change of any kind in human activity. This is because Christianity is not an ideology but a vision of the world based on Revelation which can adapt itself to any stage of human development without any problem, except the problems we create ourselves.

We must also avoid becoming so concerned with doctrinal discussions of a transcendental nature that we just never come to grips with reality. Because while Christianity is not an ideology, it is always necessary to have an ideology to put a doctrine into practice.

I think we must say, at least in theory, that it is not the role of Christianity and of the Church to develop a "Christian ideology" in very specific terms with regard to economics, politics, society, culture, or education, especially in a world which is so continuously changing. The role of the Church is rather to educate, or orientate, to contribute to an ideology which is drawn from the Christian vision of the world. But we must not identify the doctrine of Christ with very complete, concrete, definite aims in society, because these aims can be changed. There are even among Christians different opinions as to the principles and aims of society, and especially as to the different ways of achieving those aims.

I will speak to you about Latin America more extensively later on and about the role of the Church in the development of Latin America, but at this point I would like to say that I think at the present time it is necessary for the Church to go further in its action from the social point of view in Latin America. It is necessary in a developing society because of historical consequences and because of present needs.

But as we go on in a type of society where the basic problems are to orientate the society to more technical, economic, social, and cultural development, the role of the Church may be quite different. What we hope is that with the evolution of technical civilization the Church will be in a better position to perform the role of orientation in society and not one of direction, even in the ideological sphere. Not *directing*, say, that a Christian must vote for this or that party, or that he must favor this or that kind of social economic system, or that he must be a member of this or that regime, but rather giving the great principles which will *orientate* his actions in the temporal order.

A very good example of the Church's potential for orientation is found in the role that Pope John XXIII played on the international scene. The international world is no longer under the direction of the Church as it was in the Middle Ages when, for example, the Pope made the division of power between East and West (Spain and

Portugal at that time) defining the sphere of influence of each in the world. The Pope made the decision and the world accepted it. This was typical of the situation in the Middle Ages where the Church was identified with society. Of course, in our world today this kind of action by the Pope would not be heeded. But consider the impact on the world and the kind of acceptance in the world which Pope John's encyclical *Pacem in Terris* has had.

This encyclical was an act of orientation, of giving great principles, of setting forth major aims, but essentially of giving an orientation to "all men of good will." This was an action which clearly demonstrated that the Church is not seeking power in this world, but simply saying that her mission is to help people orientate themselves in the development of mankind, to point the way; that she is giving this orientation without condemnation, without any kind of temporal power or force of excommunication, but just placing this thought for the world at the world's disposal. Pope John was showing that the Church is the servant of the world, the instrument of Redemption.

However, the world reaction has been really amazing. In every part of the world the encyclical has been published; in all parts of the world, not just in the western world, but even in the communist countries. This has occurred not just because the communists could exploit some parts of the encyclical by interpreting it in their own way, but because the thoughts expressed in it are really impressive.

I was in Cuba just two days after the death of Pope John, and the government had proclaimed an official mourning of three days. But this was not so impressive to me as was the fact that the Cuban government had allowed Catholics to print ten thousand copies of *Pacem in Terris*, the only document Catholics have been permitted to publish in Cuba during the last two years. And the government requested hundreds of copies. I was told by a very well-informed person that a small study group of members of the government had taken *Pacem in Terris* privately as the subject of their weekly meetings.

This is just one illustration of how the Church can fulfill her role in present world circumstances, her work of orientation which is not really new but which the present-day evolution of the world allows her to play much more effectively than before, without going so far as to demand formal allegiance to a particular Christian ideology.

These new discoveries and the changes in the world produced by technology have brought new implications to philosophy, metaphysics, ideology. Because of the great progress that is being made in the continuing discovery of the world, it is important for us to keep abreast of these new ideas, to work realistically with them and not retreat into marginality. Technical civilization is not messianic, but it is the actual situation of man today in which we must work out the Redemption.

THE LAG BETWEEN EVOLUTION AND ORGANIZATION

We have been considering the consequences of technical civilization: changes in values, new relations between man and nature, new social relations among men, and the new empirical basis for metaphysics. The fifth and last consequence we shall consider has two aspects: the *lag between evolution and organization*, and the *lag between evolution and thought*. When I speak of evolution here I mean the *development of facts*, especially social facts, of discoveries, of the application of techniques, and so on.

Let us first look at the lag between the evolution of facts and organization, for this is one of the main problems of social life today: we are always running about after the facts without being able to catch up to them!

Take the traffic situation as an example. We have been producing more and more cars all along, but until just two or three years ago in some cities, Chicago for one, the whole organization of traffic did not begin to take care of the number of cars on the streets. What was needed to meet this evolution of traffic was better collective organization, the building of expressways, off-street parking places, and so on. This is just one example of the many, many problems we meet with today, all of which are due to the extremely rapid changes brought about by tech-

nological development. The rapidity of change increases
the lag between the time the change occurs and the time
when we can take the necessary steps to provide for it.
And this process of change will continue. It is, therefore,
increasingly necessary to provide rapid solutions to new
problems.

Another example of the lag between the evolution of
facts and the establishment of organizations needed to
deal with them is the urban situation. We have had cities
and slum and other urban problems for a number of years
now. The time we are taking to find solutions! And yet we
have the technical means at hand to solve them.

What is holding us up? Many things. Our lack of social
consciousness, for one. Our disinclination to recognize the
necessity for collective action to solve these problems,
with the result that we do not give the public authority
the necessary means to take effective action. The involved
administrative organizations for another. The administrations are so weighed down by organizational detail that
it sometimes takes years to make one decision. Also the
value system—the ideology, if you will.

I was very much impressed with the new urbanization
in the Soviet countries. In Poland, for example, where
almost all the cities were destroyed during the war, they
have been completely rebuilt. There is still a big housing
problem in the sense that people are allotted only a very
small amount of space, but there are no slums. The rate of
urbanization in Poland is about the same as that in Latin

America, but the process has been carried out very differently.

Before the war 70% of Poland was devoted to agriculture. Now less than 50% of the people, in a nation of more than thirty million inhabitants, are engaged in agriculture. This has, of course, made it necessary to build many new cities and to add extensions to the existing ones. The process has been carried out according to the rules of regional planning. There was no question of land speculation, and it was possible to build up the new workers' areas with all the necessary facilities—parks, wide avenues, schools where they were most needed, shopping centers, and so on—without difficulty. There were mistakes, but these were mistakes in planning due to lack of experience.

But it is really very impressive when we compare this with, say, the urban developments in Latin America, or with the way our own cities have grown up. With the private speculation in real estate, with the price of land so high, what is the situation of poor families in our urban slum areas? What kind of rents do they pay for substandard housing? How difficult does capitalistic speculation make it for poor families to live in decent neighborhoods with parks and other facilities?

So I have come to the conclusion that as far as the problems of urbanization are concerned, the socialist type of *organization* works better in solving them. I am not speaking of the *philosophy* of socialism but of the *organization* of collective activity to solve one specific collective problem. Socialists have not been so sucessful in other fields.

When we say that in our modern society it becomes necessary to increase the powers of government, we must be careful to understand how this is meant. Because when we speak of *socialization* we are not speaking of the power of the state to control man's free choice, his liberty of thought, of political action, of religion. This is not what socialization means. The process of socialization which we speak of and which Pope John endorsed is on the *organizational level* only, and I will try to give you an instance of how this works out in practice.

Let us take the traffic again as a very easy example. When automobiles were first in use and there were only four automobiles in one hundred square miles, we had no need for corner stop-lights, highway patrolmen, or even highways, for that matter. But now, when we have five hundred thousand cars in one hundred square miles, if we do not limit the liberty of each driver in a certain way, if we do not have some system of traffic organization, of driver licensing, etc., we make it impossible for people to use their cars at all!

So you see that organization—socialization on an organizational level—does not mean denying people their liberties but ordering social life in such a way that they will be able to exercise them. And in this sense we must modify our concept of liberty if we think of it as freedom from any kind of restraint, because we certainly must have some

limitation of our individual freedom if we are to insure
the maximum liberty of all the people.

When we consider the philosophical concept of the
liberty of man, the idea, that is, of man being more able
to become fully man, the organization of social life as it
exists in our world today actually results in an increase
of man's liberty. Who are the less free to participate in all
the advantages of social life in a technical civilization: the
people who have no car or the people who have a car and
are obliged to respect traffic regulations?

These concepts must be clearly understood if confusion
is to be avoided between the nineteenth-century "liberal"
idea of liberty and a real philosophical concept of liberty;
between *socialism* which invades the liberty of man's
thought, political action and religion, and *socialization,*
which is organization in society to serve the common good
more efficiently and to enable man to exercise his freedom
more effectively.

To return to the example of Poland. I do not say that
the people of Poland are as free in the democratic sense
as those in our western civilization. But when we analyze
the life of a Polish worker living in a good urbanized
neighborhood and compare it with the plight of the
Negro, the Mexican, the Puerto Rican in some sections of
our American cities, or with that of the worker living in
slum areas in Latin American or European cities, perhaps
we can say that the former has much freer living conditions. It may seem strange that in Poland we find a higher

percentage of urban Catholics attending Sunday Mass than in the cities of western Europe generally. In 1960 a survey was made in the city of Warsaw, now an almost completely new city of 1,200,000 inhabitants. Eighty percent of the previous population was lost in the war and the city itself was almost entirely destroyed. It has since been wholly rebuilt and is now an administrative city, very typical of the new communist middle class. The results of the survey show that 53% of the people go to Mass on Sunday. This is the highest percentage in Europe, compared with 30% in German cities, 25% in Belgian cities, 15–10% in France, and 8–9% in the great cities of Spain or Southern Italy. For North America we do not have, unfortunately, many figures. In Montreal it is 65%, and estimates for the great cities in the United States range from 80% to 30%.

I do not wish to make any further analysis of this here; I am simply introducing these facts for your consideration.

But you can see that there is a problem in the lack of collective organization which is bringing with it a decline in liberty. And this lack of organization to deal with pressing human problems is the best way to produce a kind of dictatorship on any level. When it is too late, people have a temptation to seize power by force, there seems to be no other way of making progress, and this is true from the mayor to the president of the republic.

So this lag between the evolution of the facts and the organization is really one of the great problems of today.

To a certain degree it cannot be avoided, for there is always a certain hiatus between events in society and the formation of institutions. Before any type of action can be organized and institutionalized, the facts must have developed and we must be conscious of their development. Then we must decide upon the type of organization necessary to deal with these facts and begin to institutionalize. This is why every institution, every organization, is always a little "late with the facts." *But the problem is not to be too late.* This is the great challenge to our social life today.

Because the facts are in such rapid evolution, we must always be aware of the necessity for adaptation or for creating institutions. This is true in the economy. How much technical progress is delayed because of lack of organization?

It is true in politics. Why are some administrations so inefficient in dealing effectively with the problems of urban development, with the facts of development in other countries, with the facts of economic development in general? Because so often the political administration of the whole system causes such a delay that without adaptation it ceases to be functional in meeting these new needs. It must be recognized, of course, that every institution necessary for social life has within itself a built-in effect of delaying adaptation. The more institutionalized anything becomes, the more difficult adaptation becomes. Once the constitutions are defined, once the different tasks are defined and the different competencies established, it be-

comes difficult to change all this when new definitions are
necessary. Resistance is met with on all levels.

It is true in education. The lack of adaptation of education to meet the challenge of our new scientific world is
very pronounced. But the steps needed to adapt our educational system are very difficult to take. This is because in
order to begin we must have very clear ideas about what
we wish to do, and it always seems safer to stay within a
well-defined institution than to take a step forward and
make experiments. Even now we are living in such an
institutionalized society that experimentation is very difficult; experiments in either political organization or education are not encouraged. Experiments in industry, on the
other hand, are greatly encouraged because business people have recognized that progress results from research
and experimentation. As our society requires more socialized organization the great temptation will be to institutionalize immediately in quite a few fields, to enact the
appropriate laws and statutes, and then to be in a really
difficult situation when the need for further adaptation
arises later on.

This situation is true also in the religious field. It is
one of the great problems that all our religious institutions
are facing. The fact is that we *are* in a new world, one
which is requiring new thought, new adaptation, new action, new institutions from us continuously. Yet we are so
much at ease with our well-defined constitutions, within
our well-defined spheres of action, that it is very difficult

tion"trying to see that things are going well, that everyone is at his proper place, that the organization is

for us to emerge from these into experimental fields, so difficult indeed that the people trying to meet these demands are considered misfits or nonconformists, not very well integrated into the group.

Even the authorities of the Church resist change at all levels, not only at the base—the parish, for example, or the small religious community—but even at some of the highest levels in the Church. This is the profound problem of the Council. There is great need for a "bringing-up-to-date," as Pope John said, because the Church has become so set in her institutions, yet must find new ways to meet new problems. But this should not amaze or scandalize us. The Church as an institution will always be a little late with the facts because this is a law of all institutions. The point, as I have said, is not to be too late—not to be so late that the lag between the evolution of the fact and the adaptation of the institution would render us incapable of meeting the problems.

In order to meet the problems of our rapidly changing world we must come to a new type of organization. This is true in the secular sphere also. We must see that in industry, in politics, in education. The role of the true leader is no longer one of administration, but rather one of provision and of planning. This is the great function of a leader: to lead in a prospective type of attitude. A leader in any kind of institution who is just administering the institution, trying to see that things are going well, that everyone is at his proper place, that the organization is running smoothly, is no leader in our present civilization.

Leadership in our present and ever-changing world requires the ability to see what must be done today for tomorrow, what provisions we have to make now to be ready for the work that must be done tomorrow. And really we are now in a difficult stage of transition to a new type of institution, the *evolutive* institution. Because we are living in a society where organizations are a necessity, we cannot function without them. But we are also very much aware of the inflexibility of many of our institutions and of the organizational detail which often delays action past the point where it can be effective. This is why we must develop a new type of institution, an evolutive institution, one which is not defined once and for all but is capable of development, one within which we can "institutionalize" change.

This, too, is a great challenge for the Church, because if we want her institutions to function, fulfilling her mission of being the light of this world today, we must develop evolutive institutions in the Church. Cardinal Suenens, for instance, has decided to make almost all diocesan appointments, and even national appointments of chaplains for social work, Catholic Action, of deans, and so on, for a period of only three years, after which they must be renewed. This is a type of evolutive organization, and we must have more of this sort of thinking in the Church.

Pope Paul proposed at the Council a permanent representation of all episcopates (not just those congregations defined by the Council of Trent and almost unchanged since that time) meeting at Rome regularly to consider new problems. We must come to more of this type of evolutive organization, although it will not be easy. I will go back to this idea when we begin more systematically to consider the changes in the Church's organization for action in a technological civilization.

THE LAG BETWEEN EVOLUTION AND THOUGHT

In the consideration of this time lag between the evolution of the facts of social reality and the apparatus for dealing with them, we discover that the lag occurs not only between social reality and organization but also between social reality and *thought*. This is true again in all fields.

When we think about the economic sphere, for example, we see that a great deal of our economic theory is still lagging behind the actual facts. I think this was the great merit of Galbraith's book, *The Affluent Society,* in which he showed how our economic concepts do not correspond to the new factual reality. We are always thinking in terms of an economic situation where the goods are rare. Now, on the contrary, we are living in an affluent society, a society of abundance.

In a recent book called *The Pre-Revolution*, a Brazilian economist, Celso Furtado, discussed how difficult it is to think about the reality of development because of the gap between economic *theory* and the facts, because there is a lack of theory to explain the facts. This is normal, too, to a certain degree because there is such an *acceleration* in social and technical evolution that we are bound to have some problems of lag in theory. I have talked at some length about socialization, but we had to wait so long before the concept of *socialization* in our social thought was understood as a real *technical*, and not an *ideological*, concept.

The same is true of the social aspect of development, what is now called *social change*. What is social change? We are all vaguely aware of it, are all looking for some explanation of why things are different, but as yet the whole thing has not been completely elaborated; much intellectual work remains to be done if things are to be thought through and human intelligence kept in touch with the facts.

What we must have are *engaged* intellectuals, not men who simply think beautiful thoughts having no bearing on reality. I do not say that pure research is not necessary, but we must have equally engaged intellectuals directing their thought to the actual development of humanity—not only from the spiritual point of view but from the social, the material, point of view as well. A quicker adaptation of human life to the rapid evolution of technological and social facts is especially necessary. We need teams of engaged intellectuals thinking in terms of ideas, explanations, and lines of action capable of meeting present realities. The process has to move very fast because realities are now so complex. Teamwork and more and more international co-operation are required.

This lag in thought, in theory, even in philosophy, is a fact of life not only in the secular world but also in the spiritual sphere. There is a pronounced lag between our thinking on spirituality and the world in which we are living. Think, for example, of how many of our spiritual books—and even some of the constitutions of our religious orders—are built up on this anti-intellectual basis. An anti-intellectual position was once considered a *virtue* conducive to avoiding sins of pride. We are coming out of this attitude, but it is a really typical example of our lack of adaptation in the sphere of spirituality to the needs of the modern world.

It is certain that the modern world needs as many intellectually formed persons as possible both in the Church and in secular society. We need more trained people (and more trained Sisters), intellectually speaking, who are aware of the problems of this world and capable of meeting them. The service of the Church to the world can be made very great if quite a few of our best people are used in the task of helping men adapt themselves in society.

Not only is there a lack of adaptation in our spiritual thinking, often based on anti-intellectual attitudes; there is also a *lack of integration of the whole temporal order into our spirituality*. Our vision of the temporal order is distorted by our mistaking Christ's condemnation of the sin in the world for a condemnation of the world itself.

We so often look on the temporal order as existing only for the sake of the spiritual order, or as a necessary evil to be tolerated only because it cannot be avoided. Or we consider only the spiritual life and the spiritual society as important; the rest of life has almost no value. So we have conceived what a Jesuit priest has referred to as a "spirituality of underdevelopment." And this is really true, because any concept of spirituality which does not include the development of man has forgotten or ignores the first pages of Genesis where man received from God, and not from the devil, the mission of developing the earth. This attitude has led us to forget about or to underestimate the value of the temporal order and brought about a false orientation on our part toward our lay people.

Monsignor Cardijn, coming back from the preparatory work for the Council, said that it was very beautiful what they were preparing at the Council as the role of the lay people in the Church, but it was really concerned only with the apostolate that lay people can engage in during their free time, to the neglect of what he called "the lay apostolate of the lay people."

Here again we have this idea that the whole role of the lay people in the Church is concerned with the "spiritual" side of life—what they can do in the Church, in the parish, in the spiritual society—and forgetting about all the rest! Thinking of the lay apostolate as people going from door to door inquiring into marriage cases or whether the children are going to Catholic schools, but not thinking of the role of the Christian in terms of the world or in the social development of the world. This is really a lack of spiritual adaptation to the situation of today.

In Latin America this is particularly noticeable. Among the Catholic Actionists and other groups we do find extraordinarily devout people, daily communicants, people making meditations and really living even a mystical life, but completely indifferent to all the problems of the world about them—completely marginal. The result is that this whole changing world in Latin America is now organizing itself with people who are not Catholics. It is, for example, somewhat disillusioning to find so few who are consciously Catholic present in the international organizations in Latin America. This is because they were not oriented to all these problems; these problems exist outside the type of spirituality they were formed in.

Another kind of lag in our spirituality is the inability to recognize that we are living in a mobile world. When we open some of our spiritual books, we read, for instance, that it is very difficult for those who travel a lot to sanctify themselves. And we will soon be going to the moon! This example is perhaps extreme, but at least it demonstrates that this is a mobile world. I don't say that we will sanctify ourselves just by travel! But this spirituality of immobility has to change in the world today; you have to become saints even in traveling. There is a whole range of adaptations to be made between the evolution of the social and technical facts, then, and our spirituality.

This is true also of theology. In 1962 a meeting took place in Milan with the "Sociological and Theological Approach to the Parish" as its theme. The first talk was given by a well-known theologian on the theology of the parish. He spoke very well on the classic and scholastic theology of the parish, showed how the parish was the fundamental cell of the Church, and how the whole apostolate had to be organized around the parish. But after he had finished, questions were asked, and it was pointed out that the whole concept of the parish he was describing was that of the pre-technological rural society; that these ideas dated from a time when it was possible for the pastor of the parish to know all his people, when mobility did not exist, when there were no specialized institutions, not even in the Church, for pastoral work. I must say that he was disappointed to realize that he was, in fact, using an outmoded type of sociological pattern on which to base his theological concepts, and that his conclusions were not very applicable to the reality of the parish today.

Within the last few years, theologians like Karl Rahner, S.J., and sociologists like Joseph Fichter, S.J., have reexamined the concepts of pastoral theology and parish life. Their new thought has taken into account the sociological changes of technological civilization, together with all the consequences of which I have spoken, and has related these conditions to the theological role of the parish in this type of society.

But the example above illustrates why it is so necessary today to have this sociological approach to the facts of our modern world; why we must observe what our situation actually is, in order to develop a theological approach to temporal reality. We are coming more and more to a realization that the theology of temporal reality is not a simple working out of a scheme which can be applied to any society in any time. It is becoming more evident that the real theological work today is a theological reflection on the realities. And it is only with this type of thought that we shall develop theology relevant to our mission in today's society.

There is a great need for theologians in the Church. We have many doctors of theology, but we have very few theologians. When we consider how we must apply this thinking to the role of the priest, the religious orders, the laity, the role of the North American Church, and not only for North American civilization but also for the universal Church; when we consider also the specific problems of Latin America, and the new relations of the Church with the continents of Africa and Asia, and so on, then I think we must come to the conclusion that it is absolutely necessary in all our countries, in the whole universal Church, to consecrate more of our people to this work of theological thought.

We must have a percentage of our people consecrated just to this work of discovery and to being aware of all the changes in every field. In education, in social work, in the liturgical movement, the catechetical movement, in all the specialized fields of action we need people exclusively devoted to study, to research, to thought, to experimentation in order to perform the task of theological adaptation and continuing renewal. The same thing is true for the religious life, for spirituality. Otherwise we may have a great number of Sisters in primary or secondary education, but we shall be up against it when we are confronted by these contemporary problems and unable to give an answer.

We see in the Church today how our specialized people are overworked and how often they must, in effect, beg their specialization by doing half a dozen other jobs because specialization is not yet accepted. Because there is very little financial support in the Church for their work many of our specialists must spend half or three-quarters of their time supporting an institution.

We have not yet reached the point of seeing what the real necessities are in the Church today. When we see the extraordinary possibilities for the Church and the number of consecrated people we have available to develop these possibilities, I think it would be negligent not to pursue the course of encouraging and supporting more people in specialized work, even if this meant having the courage to abandon or reduce some other kind of work in order to gain more specialized people. Not, of course, that each diocese or each congregation would have specialists in every field. This would be insupportable even if the specialists were available. But specialists from different religious orders and congregations and from the diocesan clergy could be brought together to work in these fields.

When I see, for example, the influence of very small groups of people, like the CPL, the Center for Liturgical Studies in Paris, and think of how they must work day and night and then in addition must go to parishes to preach and say Mass and so on—not as a way of keeping in touch with parish life, which would be good, but as a means of paying the rent on their office at the end of the month! Well, when I see the conditions these people work under because we are not providing the means for the Church to meet these new needs, I sometimes think we are in a state of collective sin. We should make an examination of conscience, a collective examination of conscience in our communities, to see what we can do about this problem.

What are the necessities of the Church? It is surely one of the responsibilities of our collective organizations of priests, religious, Sisters, and bishops to be aware of and try to define just what the necessities of the Church are and what kinds of new institutions and adaptations are needed to organize and direct the action of the Church in the modern world.

2 The Rapid and Continuing Process of Change

The social change accompanying the development of technical civilization is a rapid and continuing process. But not only are conditions changing, there is also an *acceleration* taking place between the process of technical discovery and the application of these discoveries in society.

A brilliant French technologist, Louis Armand, has written a book entitled *Plea for the Future*. This book contains many interesting facts about the acceleration of technical progress. Its author has just been admitted to the French Academy, the first French technologist to be so honored.

First, a few facts about this acceleration. In 1750 the annual increase in world population was 3.7 million people; in 1960, the annual increase was 45 million people. In 1700, microscopes had a magnification power of 200x; in 1960, this was 300,000x. The world production of energy in 1830 was 200 billion kilowatts; in 1960, this was 30,000 billion kilowatts. In 1830, the maximum speed was about twelve miles an hour. No danger of getting a ticket at that time! At the beginning of this century, maximum speed was 120 miles an hour; 1960 space travel goes at twenty times the speed of sound. Between the years 1860 and 1945, the strength of explosives was multiplied by 750x. When we come to the H-bomb, if we represent the power of a gun of the last century by *one*, the power of the H-bomb is 4,800,000,000 times greater!

The same acceleration is in effect in many other areas. In 1800, the world's population was consuming 4,000,000 tons of sugar; now, more than 50,000,000. In 1700, the number of stars visible to man was about 50,000; now, more than 3,000,000. The number of articles on physics in scientific journals was about 30,000 a year in 1910 and is now 240,000 a year, abstracts included. The production of plastic was zero in 1910 and is now 3,000 billion tons a year.

It is evident that we are in a process of acceleration, but what is even more amazing is the fact that there is, as I have said, an accentuated acceleration now between the time of a scientific discovery and its technical application. For example, between the discovery of the thermo-electric effect in physics and the first electric light bulb the time was thirty-five years; between the observation of X-rays and an application it was twenty years, and so on, in diminishing time lags. In fact, we could cite additional examples since the book was published, such as new methods of communication.

This brings us to one of the main conclusions which can

be drawn from our observation of the characteristics of technical civilization, a conclusion which may seem obvious but which carries with it profound implications for our thought and activity once it is really understood. It is this: not only are we now living in a state of transition, in the process of changing from a pre-technical to a technical society, in the passage from one type of civilization to another, but *we are reaching the point of living in a rapidly and perpetually changing society,* and most probably this will continue until the end of the world.

We do not, of course, know this for certain because we are not prophets. But we do know for certain that, at least for our generation, there is no chance that we shall see an end to this acceleration of new discoveries. On the contrary, now that this technical progress is of real value to people, it is becoming more and more a collective value and a social goal. In the future, co-operation among nations in the exploration of space and other kinds of international, collective action will become even more important than national achievements. Nationalism, which was the ideology of a stage in mankind's history, and which is still necessary for the normal development of the underdeveloped countries, will be replaced by more collective aims.

Because we are now living in a civilization where mutation is the normal condition of society, we must see what profound implications this has for all institutions in society, and more especially for the Church in the world today.

We must be a Church capable of living and working in a continuously changing society. We must recognize all the demands which this type of society presents to the Church, not only as to her organization, but also as to all the values we will have to develop in the Church, and all the attitudes we shall need to adopt in order to respond to this age of mankind which is sharing in the life of the plan of God, to the further development of humanity. God gave to mankind, to humanity, the mandate to discover His creation, to be master of the earth, to become more fully man, and thus in a certain sense, to be more like Himself.

There are encouraging signs that the Council will make the changes necessary for this new vision and adaptation to develop. The very fact that the Council was called, the fact that Pope John believed it necessary for the Church to adapt herself to the needs of the modern world, not only in her institutions but also in her thought, is encouraging. You know there was quite outspoken opposition among the Council Fathers on some points. And I don't see why we shouldn't admit this. After all, we are a Church of men, not of altar boys, and we should be glad of it. So there was quite some opposition in the Council just because of a lack of perception as to what the problems were. I would say the Council Fathers were divided more or less into three factions.

First, there were those who did not see that anything has changed. You may ask how this was possible, but it is so because the Church is an institution, and in any institution, even one divinely founded, it is easy after a while just to limit yourself to the origin of the institution and not to see anything else. Obviously, one of the objectives of an institution is to transmit tradition in its purity. Even so, this task itself is endangered when there is no recognition that things are changing.

Second, there were those who could see that things were indeed changing—changing so rapidly, in fact, that perhaps it would be futile or even dangerous to attempt adaptation. Adaptation or even interpretation was regarded by this faction as a danger to the truth, as a temptation of the devil. Change itself was looked upon as something evil or, at best, a matter of passing fancy, like women's fashions.

And third, there were those who were aware that things were changing in the world and were thinking of what could or should be done in the Church in order to adjust to these changes. This was the view expressed in Pope John's first speech when he said that we must distinguish between the *content* of the message we have to transmit and the *ways* in which we transmit it. The teaching does not change, of course, but every age of the Church discovers other and new *aspects* of Christ's revelation, because we live in different stages of the world's development. His message is not a dead letter, but is something living that is developing and reaching greater fullness.

Well, then, which group would prevail? There was a real danger that the Council would be too well organized by a predominantly conservative group. But because of a few minor facts—providential accidents, I would call them—the whole Council was oriented from the very beginning to another type of reaction than might have been expected.

On the first day a list of proposed members of the commissions was presented. But both Cardinal Liénart of Lille and Cardinal Frings of Cologne asked how it was possible to vote when the bishops didn't even know each other. The first meeting was over after a quarter of an hour, and the whole organization of the Council was completely changed. For two more days they had no formal meeting at all so that they could get to know each other.

In order to be able to know each other, they had to find some plan of organization, because obviously it was just impossible for 2,693 bishops to know each other individually. So the first thought was to move immediately to the organization of the Bishops' Conferences, because they knew each other by country and some of the bishops had connections with other bishops but not with all. Coming together, then, by country, they could ask each other which of the German, the French, the American bishops they knew. What was the specialty of each one? And so on.

And immediately the national conferences were working, which was one of the aims of the Council!

This brings up a small point of interest. Perhaps you remember that the Latin American bishops had the first official Continental Bishops' Conference. This was in 1955, and a permanent Secretariat of the CELAM (Council of the Latin American Bishops) was established in Bogota. When they came to Rome they asked permission to organize their Secretariat to help the Latin American bishops, but the Curia said this was not allowed because the Council was a matter for the individual bishops and not one for bishops' conferences. And yet, after the first day, the conferences were working. Not only that; after one week, the African bishops, without asking permission of anybody, announced that they had constituted a Secretariat of African bishops and had elected the African Cardinal as president with two secretaries, one English-speaking and one French-speaking. When the Latin American bishops saw this, they immediately sent a cable to the Secretary of the CELAM in Bogota asking him to come to Rome!

But what was really happening, in all these meetings and discussions and informal conferences, was a concrete living experiment. The bishops were *experiencing* the Church in her universality, because they had to meet together and inform themselves and each other of problems and situations they had never thought about before or even known to exist. And they came to a kind of discovery, a key one, which concerned *the relativity of each local Church and its situation.*

A typical example of the contrary point of view was shown by a prelate in Latin America who had spent a few years here in the United States and was so impressed with the organization of the American parochial school system that he thought this was the *only* solution to the problem of the Church in Latin America. This lack of a sense of relativity, this habit of thinking that there is only one solution to all situations, has been changed or at least modified by the discoveries the bishops made at the Council.

Their exchange of experiences has made them more progressive, more able to understand the many different types of situations now existing in the Church. Just this awareness that perhaps solutions ought to be related to particular circumstances more than we had thought is a good thing. Changes in all situations have not been immediately forthcoming, but at least we are thinking about them more realistically.

Another experience which increased the awareness of variety and relativity within the Church was the celebration of the daily Mass which took place (on different days, of course) in fifteen or so different rites. This surely brought a sense of the relativity of the Latin liturgy and a discovery, in a living way, that variety was possible within the Catholic Church.

I remember one day, particularly, when there was a

ceremony in the Ethiopian rite that was very impressive. This liturgy is inspired, musically at least, by the Arabic, and after the Mass was finished the book of the Gospels was carried in procession by the Archbishop, who had celebrated the Mass, and two other Ethiopian bishops who had assisted him. During the procession the Ethiopian seminarians sang the Credo in Bantu music with tom-toms, clapping their hands in time to the music. This was a most extraordinary experience. There wasn't another sound in the basilica.

I didn't think about it then, but afterwards the thought came to me that we were certainly being foolish in trying to replace this African music, which they already have—we didn't need to invent it—this authentic, native, beautiful music, with our Latin liturgy! Some of the other bishops felt that the African bishops were almost ready to dance.

Of course not everyone reacted so favorably. One missionary archbishop from Belgium was sitting next to an old archbishop, and he told me that every time there was a non-Latin rite Mass, this old archbishop protested, and to show his discontent he would say the rosary, aloud, in Latin, during the whole Mass!

But what is important is not so much that everyone should think exactly the same about everything, but that all of us should be aware of the existence of differing situations, of different problems, of changing cultures all capable of a vital unity "in the same spirit."

3 *Some Important Fields of Action*

22670

Our consideration of the characteristics of technical civilization: its origin as a cultural fact and its consequences—the change in social values, the new relations between man and nature and between man and society, the new empirical basis for metaphysics, the cultural lags between social reality and organization and between social reality and thought, and the fact that this world has come to a stage of rapid and continuing change—brings us to a final appraisal of *some important fields of action* before we consider the role of the Church in technical civilization directly.

I should, perhaps, take up almost every type of action of modern society, but we will instead consider just four fields: underdevelopment, leisure, education, and mass communications, because these seem to be the most important and are also some of the more typical fields of action in our modern civilization.

UNDERDEVELOPMENT

The first point, then, is the problem of *underdevelopment*. We can really say that this is the main problem of mankind today on a world basis. We have already considered this problem in some detail, so much of this will be just a quick review.

We have seen that the development of a technical civilization was primarily a matter of cultural impetus, the result of a culture placing value and importance upon research and its application. And it is a fact that this cultural evolution has taken place in western civilization. Western civilization, as a result, has assumed much of the leadership of the world, especially from the material, economic, and political points of view. And so, many of the consequences of our technical civilization have been extended to other parts of the world where our type of *culture* has *not* been extended. Thus the underdeveloped countries were brought some of the consequences of technical civilization without the cultural base from which they would normally have developed.

One of these consequences, in late years, has been the population explosion, due, in great part, to the fact that we have brought to the countries of Asia, Africa, and Latin America the application of medicine and hygiene. But the great problem arose because we accomplished these relatively easy medical advances without attempting to bring about a comparable rate of progress in the more difficult areas of economic or social development. So the lag between demographic evolution and the rate of economic, social, and cultural evolution is becoming greater and greater.

Add to this the fact that most of these countries were organized under a colonial system which made it almost impossible for them to develop their own economies, and it is not hard to see how this situation was created and made very difficult to correct.

When we consider Latin America or Africa, we see that the whole organization of economic life and social life was centered upon the needs of the mother country and not upon the development of the colony. In Latin America during the Spanish regime before the beginning of the nineteenth century, the whole economy was organized in favor of the mother country, Spain, and it was forbidden to organize industry in Latin America, or to have interregional trade. This was a monopoly of the mother country. All international trade had to go through the harbor of Cadiz in Spain.

This same type of exploitation took place also in Africa. In very recent years some countries in Africa have assumed social and educational responsibilities, but the whole organization of their economic life has been determined by the industrial, metropolitan mother countries. And when, in Latin America, these countries got political independence, they did not get economic independence along with it; the same profit, or more, has been transferred from Spain to North America.

In order to allow the underdeveloped countries to begin to compete in the world economy, some kind of balanced arrangement between them and the more developed and industrialized countries will have to be worked out. The underdeveloped countries are providing the raw materials or the agricultural products needed for manufacturing in the industrialized countries. And since over a period of, say, a century there has been a cyclic tendency for the prices of raw materials and all the agricultural products of the underdeveloped countries to *go down,* and at the same time, owing to technological advances, a corresponding *increase* in industrial products and wages, a point has been reached where the demographic pressure in the underdeveloped countries and the increased pressure of rising social consciousness have combined to render their whole situation intolerable.

We have considered the fact that with the extension of communications, geographical and ideological, we no longer live in isolation from any other part of the world. We are living on the world base in a pluralistic society. And this is just as true of the underdeveloped countries. The social consciousness of these people is rising in a very rapid way because of this extension of communications. And a condition that was once bearable because it was all that was known has now become psychologically intolerable in comparison with the now-known conditions in the technically developed countries of the rest of the world.

The great increase of nationalism among the African and Latin American countries is an indication of this feeling. We may perhaps think that many of the African countries would be far better off under British, French, or Belgian administration. But this condition was not possible any longer because of the psychological pressure of social consciousness. And their nationalism, if it is turned in the right direction, can be a tremendous force in helping the people develop their own countries. The problem of underdevelopment, however, cannot be solved by either the developed countries or the underdeveloped countries alone. It is really a world problem which will require united effort and support.

I have told you in a simplified way of the *why* behind the need for action in the field of underdevelopment. Much more could be said, and we will continue to make references to this problem.

What, then, are the *characteristics* of the underdeveloped countries? We will consider just a few, because many of them are generally known.

First of all, it is a fact that *underdevelopment is a relative concept*. We ourselves are underdeveloped by comparison, say, with the society of 1980. It is the *consciousness* of the *vast* contrasts between the underdeveloped countries and the more developed ones even in their present relative development that is creating one of the great problems in today's world. Of course we shall always have some differences in degree of development between various countries, but this does not necessarily produce problems because the contrasts are not ordinarily so great.

From the economic point of view, for example, it is true that the United States is more highly developed than Europe, but there has never been the problem between Europe and the United States which now exists between the underdeveloped and the developed countries because the difference has not been so great.

Of course the main difficulty in redressing the economic lag is the fact that technological progress, and especially the accelerated technological progress necessary to bring the underdeveloped countries up to the level of the developed, is only possible when there is already some degree of prosperity. It is only where the capacity for investment in research and industry exists that this progress can be achieved. And the capacity does not exist in the developing countries.

If anything, the gap appears to be widening. Whereas just a few years ago these countries were barely meeting their basic needs, now the increase of population is absorbing whatever gains have been made in development, with the result that the actual difference between the developed and the underdeveloped countries is increasing.

It has been calculated that the standard of living was 15 times greater in the United States than in India before the war in 1939; in 1950, it was about 35 times greater. This difference affects not only the present standard of living but also the future possibilities of these countries. This has had very great psychological consequences because the people are now conscious of these differences; before the war they were scarcely aware of them.

The second characteristic of the underdeveloped countries, and an important one for us to remember, is the immense importance of the *cultural* factor. This is not to say that some cultures are "higher" or "better" than others in the moral sense; we use the word "culture" in the same sense as we have used it before—as an expression of social values. Technical civilization is a cultural fact which resulted from the values of western civilization. And in order to develop technological civilization among the underdeveloped countries, a change in their culture must take place, in their attitudes toward nature, toward life, toward time.

We could ask why it is necessary to extend technical civilization to these people. They are very happy with their own concept of time, with their cultural approach to life and to nature. Why must they change all this? Maybe they don't want to change. This is very true. But we forget that a tremendous change has already been brought to these people with the demographic evolution. It is impossible to go backwards. They must also have the possibility of solving this problem, and this will require technical development.

Technical development is possible, however, only with

the acceptance of some aspects of the cultural values of technical civilization. This is why we have radio schools in Colombia and other parts of Latin America. Their purpose is not so much to teach the people to read and write as it is to change their cultural attitudes. These attitudes would persist, you know, even with new methods of agriculture. Sometimes it has been said that if we just sent technicians to these countries, the problem would be solved. Well, we can send technicians with their knowledge of the newest and most productive methods of agriculture, but they must still work with the *people*. And if these people have not changed their cultural attitudes in some respects, the technicians will get nowhere.

Remember the story of the Colombian peasant, hesitating between the blessing or the fertilizer? This difficult problem of attitude does exist. I remember another example which illustrates this point.

The representatives at one of the first FAO conferences in Mexico were talking about a new kind of hybrid corn which had a very high rate of productivity. They were trying to get the farmers of Mexico to use this corn and had met with tremendous resistance. The Mexican peasants simply did not want it. Monsignor Ligutti, the founder of the Catholic Rural Life Conference of the United States and permanent observer for the Holy See at the FAO, told them why. He stood up and said, "If you don't know peasants, you cannot work with peasants.

What you must do is give this corn a name. Call it San Isidro corn, and you will see what happens."

The people at the meeting thought the good priest must be joking. After all, this was an international conference, and he should at least be serious about such important problems!

But the members from Mexico understood the lesson and adopted his idea. The corn was named "San Isidro Corn," and in two years the production had doubled. Now this was a cultural solution. I don't say that there is a cultural solution for all mankind's problems, but a cultural understanding does help.

The third characteristic is that there are *great lags between the different areas of development*. The greatest, and the most important, is the lag between population expansion and the economy. This is basically the same situation we discussed when we were speaking of the way our institutions, our organizations, and even our thoughts are lagging behind the evolution of social facts.

But here the lag between the social facts and the organization to deal with them is most dramatic because we are faced with tremendous problems. People are starving, dying of hunger, not because the earth cannot yield enough food to feed the population, but because our economy and our international institutions are so badly organized. And we have a grave international responsibility to help these people.

When we take, for example, the total expenditures for

arms by all the countries of the world, both east and west, we have an amount of 120 billion dollars a year. When we put together all the help for the underdeveloped countries in the world, coming from America, Europe and also Russia, the total is less than 10 billion dollars. Actually, the maximum is about 6 billion dollars. About three years ago, it was only around 3½ billion.

When this figure is compared with the collective amount spent on armaments—120 billion dollars a year—we can see that we are living in a world where things are not going exactly right.

We can appreciate the importance of the move towards disarmament in the world because obviously we cannot set aside so much money for armaments and at the same time increase the aid for economic solutions. The technical means exist to solve the problem of underdevelopment, but *this is a collective task*. In order to accomplish it we must make many changes in our international co-operation. If we could reduce the amount of money spent on armaments and put some of this money toward the development of the underdeveloped countries, it would be one part of the solution.

Another step is a regulation of prices on the international market. This of course will be a difficult step, especially in a capitalistic system which is keyed to competition and to getting the greatest return for the least possible investment. But some regulation in prices is necessary in order to allow the underdeveloped countries to realize a good basis for planning.

President Kennedy understood this very well and commented upon the problem clearly about two years ago. He stressed the necessity for the developed, industrialized countries to come to international agreements with the underdeveloped countries on prices on the international market. Countries like Colombia, for example, whose income depends upon the prices of one or two products, cannot make plans for development because they cannot tell what their income for the following year will be. They have very little to say in the matter. Their incomes are decided, practically speaking, by the industrial countries which are determining the prices on the international market. And a beautiful plan for expansion or development can be made, but if the next year the price of coffee goes down one or two cents a pound, this affects the whole economy.

I told you about the decreasing prices for raw materials and the increase in prices for industrial products. This means that the underdeveloped countries have relatively less income from their own products and have to pay more to buy the industrial products outside. In fact during the years between 1955 and 1960, prices on the international market were so low that the loss of income of the underdeveloped countries on the international market was greater than all the foreign aid these countries received. So they lost more money than was given to them by the

industrialized countries for development. We can say
that we gave a few billion dollars in aid, but we actually
gained many more billions of dollars because of the
decrease in the prices we paid for raw materials and
agricultural products.

Another point to be considered in the solution of underdevelopment is that we must come to more international
and collective types of action, rather than bilateral agreements. The bilateral arrangement can be a way of maintaining a kind of colonial system in practice if not in
theory. Not all bilateral aid is bad, of course not; it is
sometimes helpful to have some control over the use of
the money given. But in general we must use more multi-
lateral arrangements which will help us avoid the temptation to exercise power because we have given aid.

It is necessary, also, to allow the underdeveloped countries to exercise some kind of control on the use of the
funds allocated to them for development. In this sense, the
Alliance for Progress was surely a very good step in the
right direction. I don't believe that the realization of the
plan has been perfect, but the idea of bringing together
these countries and giving them some control over the
utilization of funds is very useful. And I do think that
this is the only way of exerting a real control on the funds
for these countries. For at the present time, at least, many
of these governments represent only a small percentage of
their people, and are often maintained for personal ad-

vantage and not for the interests of all. These officials, seeking personal advantage, generally insist that the money be given directly to the government without any condition and without any control.

This will not work. In some countries of Latin America money from the Alliance was used to make the rich richer, but little was used for development. With the rise of nationalism, it is easy for the government to justify its aversion to any kind of control by appealing to the people's sense of national pride. "These people who are trying to help us want to control our economy, our social life, and our political life," they say. And of course there is some element of truth in this. The fact, however, that there are conditions of social reform, such as land reform and educational reform, set by the Alliance for Progress is an indication of a more realistic approach to these problems.

If there were international organization of all these countries, however, and if those countries receiving aid had a measure of control over each other in the utilization of the technical assistance and the funds which were given, this money would be put to better use.

Much more could be said about the problems of the developing countries. But the fact remains that much of the great problem of underdevelopment was brought about, not by technical civilization as such, but because we conducted our progress in such a way that these conditions were an accompanying result.

There is an additional reason for the Church and for Christians, especially, to be aware of this problem. It is a fact that underdevelopment is the primary world problem today; it is also a fact that the majority of the world's Christians live in the one-third of the world that is developed. If we, therefore, do not accept a major responsibility for helping to solve this problem, *this will be one of the greatest scandals of the modern world: that Christians did not take the responsibility.*

EDUCATION

We have already discussed the role of education to some extent and we shall not go into this at great length here, but I would like to take the time to consider briefly a point or two in this very important field of action.

In such a changing world, in a civilization as technically developed as ours, the aspect of education as a process of socialization is becoming more important. Education can be viewed from two aspects: as a formation of the individual personality and as a process of socialization. As a socialization process it means the development of a person in the ways which will enable him to participate in a given society, understanding and recognizing the needs and responsibilities of the world in which he lives and able to exercise successfully his social rights and responsibilities. And this aspect of education is especially important in a complex society such as ours in which collective forms of action are becoming of increasingly critical necessity.

Our Catholic education for the most part is really very much behind the times so far as the emphasis on social values is concerned. We have attached such importance to the formation of personality that we are, in a sense, almost dysfunctional in a socialized world, because we are not forming people able to act in the kind of society in which they are living. The development of personality is important, of course, but man exists in society, and this aspect of his education must not be neglected. I won't go further into this, but you can see the kind of thought which can be given to this situation.

We must re-examine and revise when necessary, not so much our program of courses, as all the values we say we are transmitting in our Catholic education. I think we must examine especially the latent values we are conveying through our educational system, to see whether we are actually educating people to live and work in this world or whether we are helping Christians to remain marginal in this type of civilization.

What is it to be marginal? To be regressive, to insist on such attitudes and values as are completely opposed to any kind of collective values because we have mistakenly identified socialization with socialism. All the consequences of technological civilization are such that they require collective action to organize and develop the potentialities they involve. A Catholic educational system which ignores the broader implications of social responsibility will produce disengaged, marginal Christians rather than the engaged intellectual leaders capable of integrating technical civilization with the Christian vision.

We have been referring to the educational system in our own developed countries. When we speak of educating the people of the underdeveloped countries to the values of technical society, I don't mean that we have to impose our own culture upon them. This would be completely wrong. Yet it is happening, especially in the countries which are aware of having achieved a good synthesis between cultural values and technical civilization. The great temptation is to try to bring the same kind of synthesis to all the people of the developing countries. This is wrong because it is not our way of life we are to bring to them, not the American way of life nor the European way of life. We are there to help them to discover the technical means and values necessary for development; they must make their own synthesis between their cultures and the technical advances.

For example, we are living in a technical civilization in the United States, in Canada, in Europe. But we still have many differences. The way in which the Germans or the French or the North Americans have integrated technical civilization with their own culture is quite different. We see how the Italians are adding a dimension of what can only be called "style" to their industrial development, their factories, their bridges, their automobiles. The prestige body-designs for automobiles are made by Italians. They are really making a cultural contribution to technical civilization, one of emphasis on the aesthetic aspect of industrial products and production. The same thing is true of the Czechs and the Scandinavians. Aesthetic values brought to industrial production, making very simple things for daily life, but functional, practical, beautiful.

So this synthesis of technical civilization with individual cultures is something for each country to achieve; it is not to be imposed upon the people from without.

For practical purposes in our teaching and educational institutions, it might perhaps be useful to include a course in cultural anthropology, but only if the course concentrated on the structural changes in the culture of man in a technical civilization, rather than on some detailed study of, say, some specified Indian culture. In other words, cultural anthropology studies the broad areas of urban, technical living and of rural, non-industrial, pre-technological life in order to assess the reasons for the differences in cultural backgrounds, and to understand the structural changes involved in the process of development from the one type of society to the other.

But it is necessary for all our education to include the development of social values along with personality values, so that educated Christians shall not absent themselves from the very society they are meant to inform.

LEISURE

The field of leisure activity presents a third important area for consideration. With the development of technical civilization we are coming, perhaps more rapidly than we think, to a civilization oriented toward leisure. The first step in the technical society was industrial and based on work; in a civilization oriented toward leisure, work will be valued as a means toward leisure.

We do not speak of leisure in the sense of just doing nothing, but in the sense of the free activity of man. Leisure is not the opposite of work, but it is the opposite of obligatory work.

One of the great problems in education is that we are educating children with methods and values of yesterday, yet they will live tomorrow. One of the aspects of tomorrow is that these children will be adults in a leisure type of civilization, and we must form them to the extent that they will be able to make their way in this culture and not be at a loss to adjust. Of course we already know that there are great lags because people will take some time to become accustomed to a leisure civilization.

The sphere of leisure offers great advantages, I think, from the religious standpoint. In Europe apostolic work in resorts and other vacation areas is beginning to be organized, and the experience of priests and lay people in it is most encouraging. They all say it is amazing how much more open and approachable people are during their leisure time. It is much easier to talk with them, to bring them to some kind of awareness of spiritual matters, because they are free. This does not happen automatically, of course, but we must apply ourselves to this area, working out new types of apostolic organizations to meet with people in their leisure time. Our present organizations are not geared to this activity.

There are now great possibilities open to people in their leisure time for religious education, for lectures, conferences, discussion groups and for many other religious activities which were simply not possible before because the whole day or the whole year was spent in obligatory activity.

The potentiality exists, then, for very great development of religious activities in this new type of civilization, and we must prepare ourselves to take part in this development.

THE MASS MEDIA

Finally, we come to the mass media. This field is very important because a great part of our culture is now formed through mass communications. This will, in the years to come, revolutionize many aspects of our lives. The field of education, for example, will be greatly influenced when we are able to receive as many as a thousand channels on one television set. It will be possible to develop teaching through television much more completely and effectively than we have now.

In the future mass communications will serve as the great instrument for the transmission of social values and of culture. The consequences of this for the transmission of religious values will be immense, and yet we are still mere children so far as implementing the possibilities is concerned. We have developed the techniques of radio and television so little that our transmission of religious values has been generally ineffectual if not altogether primitive.

Until now our use of these media has been directed toward publicizing the activities we are already engaged in, putting a sermon on the air or televising the Mass. We have seldom utilized their full potential by adopting their proper techniques and working creatively within the wide scope they afford. A vast amount of work remains to be done in this field.

But even with this brief survey of all these fields of action, we can see how many possibilities there are for organized action in the technical civilization which is present and growing all around us, in the changed and changing world in which we are living.

With all this in mind, then, we shall now turn our attention to the specific role of the Church in our technical civilization.

PART TWO

The Church in
Technical Civilization

"We desire to win the age. Let us not, then, stand
isolated from it. Our place is in the world as well
as in the sanctuary; in the world, wherever we can
prove our love for it or render it a service. We
cannot influence men at long range; close contact is
needed. Let us be with them in the things that are
theirs—material interests, social welfare, civil weal
—so that they may be with us in the things that are
ours, the interests of religion. Let us be with them
because their interests are ours, and ours are theirs,
because nature and grace must not be separated."

—ARCHBISHOP JOHN IRELAND

The Church in
Technical Civilization

When we refer to the new relations between the Church and the world, we mean more specifically the Church as an *institution* facing the problems of the evolving technical civilization. Of course we cannot make an essential distinction between the Church as an institution and the Church as the Mystical Body of Christ; all we can do is look at the attitudes of Christians in the modern world. We have already made quite a few general applications to the Church in our consideration of the development and consequences of technical civilization; we shall now consider problems related more specifically to the institutional aspects of the Church.

The consequences of technical civilization are seen in five major areas: the new relations between the Church and the world; the new organizations in the Church; new types of action; new roles; new thought. We shall see how all these changes in the world have brought a new look to the Church in quite a few respects: in the spheres of thought, organization, and action. And this, you see, is coming nearer and nearer to the great "why" of the Council.

4 The New Relations between the Church and the World

The relations between the Church and the world today are influenced by several factors. The first one we shall consider is the problem of the number of Catholics in the world and how this affects missionary activity.

NUMBER OF CATHOLICS AND
MISSIONARY ACTIVITY

Whether we are speaking of the Catholic Church as an institution or thinking of it in terms of membership, we must take into account the proportionate number of Catholics in the world today in our thinking about the mission of bringing the Kingdom of God to the whole world. The fact is that since the First Vatican Council the proportion of Catholics in the world has not changed. We had then, and we have now, about 19%. And if we project our calculations into the future, to the year 2000, the most optimistic figure we can arrive at is 15% or 16%.

This figure of course depends upon the kind of base on which we calculate statistics. We arrive at it by looking at the population explosion of the non-western peoples in the underdeveloped countries. The majority of the world's Catholics live in the developed countries where the birth rate is decreasing slightly. So, with the exception of Latin America, which now has 8% of the world population and will have a slightly higher percentage in a few years, the great increase in population is taking place in the countries with a very small percentage of Catholics. This is why, with the population trend continuing as it is today, by the year 2000, Catholics will be only about 15% or 16% of the world's population.

This first point concerning the number of Catholics in the world brings us to a new reflection: we are living in a world where we are becoming a smaller minority. And of course we have to think in terms of the world and not just of the situation in our own country. This fact is calling forth some really new and challenging questions with regard to the concept of the Church's mission in the world.

It may be that at times our whole missiology, our whole approach to the extension of God's kingdom, has been too simplistic. There are theologians who are thinking that perhaps the mission of the Church in the world is, and will be till the end of time, always to be a minority; to be only this seed that Christ brought into the world, which will germinate and grow to the dimensions of a great tree, but perhaps not in this world. Well, you can see all the questions this idea is raising. Maybe it is too radical. And there are, of course, other theologians thinking in another direction.

But at any rate it is impossible in the present world to think only in numerical terms when we consider the Church's mission. We must think more in terms of quality than of quantity. And when we see the conditions of Catholicism in the social change of Latin America, when we see the problems of the Church in the new African countries and in Asia, I think we must not become too optimistic about great numerical increase in the future.

Our concept of the Church's mission in the world must be revised in terms of world conditions. I do not say that we must be less missionary, that we need no longer consecrate a great number of our priests, Sisters, Brothers and lay people to be missionaries to other civilizations, to non-Christian countries. We must, of course, continue to do all this. But the kind of work which has to be done now is much more a work of orientation, in keeping with Pope John's thought, without an aggressive, proselytizing attitude; we have more the mission of orienting mankind in this difficult time of social change and the expansion of technical civilization. This may not necessarily mean the immediate individual conversion to the Church of millions of people, but it will surely mean a greater presence of

Christ in the world, because it will be a sign of love which is bringing people of good will nearer to God.

So you can see that even though all theologians are not yet in clear agreement about every aspect of this question—we are just beginning to explore some new ideas—still it is certain that we must abandon the concept of the mission which was that of the Crusade, or the concept of the mission which was identified with the colonial type of action by western countries in Asiatic and African countries, and develop some other kind of thinking with regard to our mission work in the world.

We must come to an approach which will take into consideration all these processes of evolution in the world: the fact of world unity through communication; the fact that we are living in a pluralistic world with the consequence of necessarily respecting the attitudes and beliefs of others (an attitude which is in the final analysis more evangelical than any other); the fact that problems are now collective problems for all mankind to solve and that we need orientation and guidance which will be really helpful to mankind in solving these problems.

As I have said, it is really extraordinary how the action of Pope John was accepted by the world because it was of this sort—not imposed from an attitude of power, but simply from an attitude of love and a wish for better orientation. Perhaps all missionary activity in the world will have to be much more along this line, and much less concentrated on the numerical, quantitative approach.

We think, for instance, of the evangelization of Latin America. It is false to say that this was achieved only by force, but certainly it was completely integrated with the whole concept of "Hispanidad," which was linked with the concept of "Christianidad" in a very strange mixture of spiritual and very temporal aims. It is plain that our mission work in Africa was very much linked with colonial power, and in a certain way was very helpful to the colonial powers. Not in a completely wrong way, not in an immoral way, but in such a way that the colonial system had all the advantage of having missionaries assume the responsibility of many of the social, educational, and health services for the population.

Of course this also gave the missionaries some advantage in that they had a kind of monopoly on these services. This, in effect, gave them an instrument of power, and a means of attracting converts not solely by the exercise of charity but often in view of too human considerations. We must be very frank about this, although it is also true to say that most missionaries were not at all consciously using this power or even perhaps aware of it. But it was there. And when the events of the Congo came along a few years before this country achieved independence, and when the prestige of the whites was disappearing, it had a real influence on the number of conversions.

Certain tribes turned to Catholicism or Protestantism for very natural reasons. In Rwanda, for example, between the two wars, there was a tremendous number of

conversions among the Watusi. This was the leading tribe
of Rwanda. At first they resisted all the influences of
Christianity, because they had a very highly developed
culture and a sense of superiority. But then after a few
years, when they saw that the other tribes, the lower
classes of their society, were, as a result of the education
they received at the mission, beginning to rise in some
functions even in the colonial system, they understood
why. As a result, there were enormous numbers of conversions to Christianity. Many of these people really became good Christians, but of course for many others it
was a very human kind of motivation which brought about
the conversion, especially among the chiefs. At the time
there was little attention to the sociological interpretation
of this development—it was spoken of as a "tornado" of
the Holy Ghost.

Human factors will always play a role in the development of the Church because God is working in the world,
but motivation for conversion must be or become supernatural.

And so the question remains: What is the role of the
Church in the modern world? We have on the one hand
the mission from Christ to bring the Gospel to the utter-
most ends of the earth. On the other hand we see that
the number of Catholics, and of Christians in general, is
actually decreasing in the world because of the population
trend. When we try to make prospectives, we find
it is very probable that among most Asian and African

peoples we shall have even greater difficulty in making conversions in the future. We see also that in Latin America we may have to expect a Christianity which is gaining enormously in quality, but suffering a proportional loss in quantity.

In view of these facts, then, perhaps it might be well to re-examine our previous somewhat simplistic numerical attitude toward missionary activity, to think less in terms of immediate conversion to the visible Church and more in terms of meeting those of other religions in a truly Christian ecumenical spirit.

This ecumenical approach, despite a possible risk of relativism, is not a relativist attitude. But this new spirit, which is now growing among Christians and between Christians and Jews, will probably be the same one which we shall have to adopt toward the Moslems and the other great religions of the world.

Make no mistake about this. I am not saying that we are to interpret the mission to "Go and baptize all nations" merely in a mystical or allegorical sense. Surely not. But we must come to a better idea from the theological point of view of what is meant by this command.

Of course the normal way for salvation is by baptism in the Catholic Church. And we believe that. But there are three observations to make, at least, about how we are to carry out this mission.

The first one: What are the *means* we are using to bring people to ask for baptism? Because what Christ asks of us is not to force people to baptism, not to use powerful inducements to bring people to baptism, but to propose it to people in such a way that they will ask for it. *We sometimes forget that it is not we who are converting people, but God.*

I remember a conversation with a political leader of a European country not long ago; he was telling me of a conversation he had held with a bishop of this same country. The bishop was speaking of Christians in the world and of the lay apostolate, and he said, "Every time I see a layman I ask him, How many people have you tried to convert?" Well, this man reacted very strongly to this. He said, "Your Excellency, I thought that God was the one doing the converting!"

He went on to tell me that his secretary had become a Catholic after two years of working for him, but that he had never tried to convert the man. And when he announced that he was joining the Catholic Church, his employer's first reaction was to ask, "Did you think freely about this?" His secretary said, "I thought you would be very pleased." And the political leader answered, "Yes, I am pleased, but only if you think in your own conscience that this is the thing for you to do. In that case, of course, I am very happy." Then he asked his secretary when he had first thought of becoming a Catholic and the man said, "Since I came to work for you."

So you see, this layman did not "try to convert." For a long time he did not even know that his secretary was a Protestant. But through his way of living he brought the question to the man's mind. That is just an example of the first point, the ways we are using to bring people to baptism.

A second consideration is the way in which we use those evangelical methods. It is not that we must say nothing about our faith, it isn't that. It is a matter of not being *aggressive* about the conversion of other people—which is surely not, I think, evangelical. Also, through not being aggressive we leave up to God the time for a man's real conversion. We are not masters of time, God is, and He knows when He will give the grace of conversion. What we have to do is to give the *opportunity*, to present our faith, and to do this with an attitude of love, not of aggression. And the utilization of human power for the benefit of making conversions is a real aggression.

The third consideration has reference to the collective aspect of Christianization. In a world which is so socialized, the transmission of cultural, moral and religious values is made not only by the individual action of one person toward another, but also by the attitudes we as a group are taking in society, by our *collective testimony*. When Pope John wrote *Pacem in Terris* this was really an extremely profound religious act, a missionary action, but perhaps he did not bring one individual man to ask for baptism. His action was a collective one.

Or as another example, the pastors of one neighborhood

in Paris brought to the newspapers a joint declaration protesting the treatment given to the North Africans in that neighborhood. This was collective action bringing to the attention of the public certain moral values, certain Christian values.

Or again, the example of Archbishop Botero Salazar of Medellin, Colombia, whose family built him a large "palace" on a hill just above the city in a kind of medieval symbolism (the bishop being the prince of the city). He understood that this was really a wrong attitude for a bishop in an underdeveloped country, and he just turned over the finished "palace" to make a school to train labor leaders. He then chose to go and live in a workers' neighborhood in a very simple house. This, also, was not an act of conversion of one person with regard to another, but an act which had a collective meaning. As it turned out, this action became known not only in his own city, but throughout Latin America, and indeed it was published all over the world. But you see what Christian values are being shown forth here: the concern of the Church for the poor, and the abandoning of an attitude of power and domination.

All these actions, then, have had great missionary significance. So we must be attentive to the collective approach of our apostolate. And when we say that we are to go and baptize all nations, we must remember that this means not only to propose the Faith to individual persons, but also to perform the kind of actions which really can help the world toward an awareness of human values, moral values, spiritual values, trusting that they will finally discover, if this is the will of God, the essential value of the Church as the intermediary for salvation.

THE NEW CONTINENTS:
AFRICA AND ASIA

The second factor in the new relations between the Church and the world is the meeting with the new continents, notably Africa and Asia. Of course these are not new continents in the literal sense; their civilizations are even much older than ours. But it is a new encounter for the Church.

It can be said that the Church has been present for centuries in Africa and also in Asia. Yes, but what kind of presence? This is the whole problem. If we look at a map of the world, we see that the only countries in Asia where Catholicism is present in terms of numbers of people are the Philippines, Vietnam, the South of India, and a few other places. In the rest Catholics are very, very small minorities. And this corresponds exactly with the colonial expansion of the Latin countries. Within the last fifty years there have been other influences from the Catholic point of view in Asia, but for the most part there is an almost identical similarity between colonial influence and Catholicism.

With the emergence of the new continents, and by this I mean the continents having a new national and new continental *self-consciousness,* we are coming to a sense of the very great cultural distance which exists between the Church and these cultures. The fact that Catholicism is so closely identified with western culture is creating an even greater barrier than existed before the growth of the strong sense of nationalism which accompanied the achievement of independent status by the former colonies of the western world.

To give you a similar example in Europe. When we look at a map of Germany before the division of Germany and the great movement of refugees, we see that the Catholic regions of Germany corresponded almost exactly to the frontiers of penetration of the Roman Empire, and that the break-up following the Reformation followed along those same lines. This indicates that the problem of the Reformation was not simply a theological problem, but was also very much linked with cultural and social backgrounds. Because there is no question that with time the Church tends in a normal way to become identified with the culture of the people; it is not something which just exists there a few feet above the ground! But of course if there is a complete identification, there is great danger to the universality, the spiritual transcendence of the Church.

This problem exists, to a much greater extent, in Asia and Africa. Sometimes people wonder why the Church does not make more progress among the Moslems, especially in North Africa. And sometimes it is said that the missionaries, the White Fathers, did not use a good method. Or that they abandoned the field too rapidly. I have heard this said and seen it printed.

But the truth of the matter is that the Moslem religion is very closely linked with the culture of the people, especially with Arabic culture. And for them the Christian religion, especially the Catholic religion, is as closely linked with western culture as Islam is with Arabic. The result is that while, at present, they do not have a particularly hostile attitude toward Christianity (although there are signs that hostility is increasing in parts of Africa), they do think that Christianity is the religion of western people. And they have their own.

The Church appears to them to be something completely foreign to their culture. It would be most abnormal for an Arab of North Africa to be called a Christian; it would seem like a contradiction in terms. The few Arabs who are converted to Catholicism have to leave Tunisia, Algeria, Morocco, not because they would be persecuted as Christians but because they are considered traitors to their culture. Since they have chosen the religion of western civilization, they must leave; there is no longer any place for them. And of course as long as the Church continues to present itself to the Arabs of North Africa as something completely foreign, as long as they think that to become a Christian means to abandon their Arabic culture, then there is little chance of any kind for conversion, or even for dialogue.

For the last thirty years or so, the White Fathers have been working at the IBLA, the Institute of Arabic Literature. Their studies have concentrated on Arabic literature and other aspects of Arabic culture, and they have become such experts that they are considered in Tunisia as the people who have been able to bring a clearer definition to the new Tunisian culture. This is, of course, an outstanding contribution to a new country.

I don't think this particular group of White Fathers has ever converted, or tried to convert, one Tunisian, but what they have accomplished in the way of dialogue contributing to the growth of new understanding, in raising certain questions in the minds of the people—here were Christians who were able to enter so fully into the native Arabic culture that they helped to define it—the value of this contribution in terms of the mission of the Church is very great.

So there are many problems which we now have to meet with the rise of national consciousness in these new countries and continents. And very often we are far from having the right attitude or the means to meet these people and to incarnate Christianity outside the western world. Many of the young African bishops (not so much the Asian bishops—they were generally more conservative) came to the Council so full of the most extraordinary dynamism, and with such strong views about their many concrete problems, that they even brought a little alarm to the Curia!

But the point is this: to meet the culture of these people and to work within it we are going to have to make many changes in the Church, especially in our attitude and approach toward other cultures. I remember, for example, a story told me by one of the leaders of the Legion of Mary in France.

This man had been sent on an economic mission in Communist China by his banking organization. When he got to Peking, of course, he toured the city with a guide. The tour went on all day. At night they came to the city square where the Catholic cathedral stood. Here was this neo-Gothic structure, illuminated by floodlights—this in a communist country. The man was astonished, and he asked the guide why it was done. The guide told him to go up and take a closer look. After looking around and seeing nothing out of the ordinary, he turned to the guide again. Well, just look at that statue there," the guide said. The tourist looked at the big floodlit statue. "It's either St. Michael or St. George, but I don't see anything unusual about it."

So the guide told him. "You see that, the statue of a young white man beating the dragon? Well, this is the symbol of what the western countries have done to China. The dragon is the symbol of China, and the white man is the symbol of the western countries. And this is why we are illuminating the cathedral—to be a constant reminder to the people of what you have done to us."

This is what can happen when we bring our symbols unchanged into another country's culture, when we make no real effort to understand their symbols and customs, but unhesitatingly seek to impose our own. Of course many, many stories like this can be told.

Since before the war, the episcopate in Japan has been composed wholly of Japanese, and not long ago I was talking with a Japanese bishop who was visiting in Brussels. And he said, "You know, I have a great sorrow. Because of my whole formation"—he was trained in Rome and had traveled extensively in Europe—"I feel much more at home here in Europe than in my own country."

So we are now facing many new problems of *attitude* in all the activities of the Church. For example, when we think about the necessity for great adaptations if our liturgy is really to communicate with these people. It is strange to observe that in many countries of Africa and Asia the native clergy, with a few exceptions, are much more conservative than the missionaries on some of these questions. This is especially true of the first generation of the native clergy. And I think it is a direct result of the kind of formation we have given them. They have been educated in such a way that they are not able to distinguish between the essence of the message and the forms in which it is given. And so, to be sure of not losing the essentials, they are integralists; they want to keep everything in the exact form in which it has been given and are in a bad position when it comes to adaptation.

Of course in the second generation of the native clergy, especially in Africa, we already find people who are much better trained, more able to think in terms of adaptation in the liturgy, in canon law, in all spheres of ecclesiastical discipline.

All this thought is not really so revolutionary because we already have the Eastern rites in the Church. Their ecclesiastical discipline and their liturgy are very different. Among the Maronites, for example, we have the liturgy in the vernacular. We have married priests in all the Eastern Churches; we have deacons. We have all kinds of institutions that we do not have in the Latin Church. So why should we be so hesitant about going along some of these same lines for these new countries?

One objection, of course, will be raised immediately: the question of unity. Because, as I noted earlier on, one of the great factors (and perhaps a greater one than we have thought) in all the schisms in the Church has been *cultural* rather than theological. So the idea that the Church should diversify herself more and more along the lines of different cultures does present a possible danger, a limitation, to a certain extent, of her universality.

But we don't have to confuse essentials and think that to maintain the universality of the Church we must impose universally just one way of doing things. Or to think of unity merely in terms of one form of unity—the unity of centralization, or a cultural unity with Latin, as some documents erroneously state, as *the* language of the Church. This is completely wrong from the theological point of view. One of the Russian observers at the Council said, "We know that we are a local Church and we could wish that the Latin Church would recognize that she is too."

Universality is possible only if Christianity is able to penetrate and to become integrated with all cultures. And unity now, in these days, can be thought of in an entirely different way than a few years ago because of the new forms of communication in the world. These have had a tremendous impact on ecclesiology. It would be very interesting to write a treatise on the influence of communications on the Church.

The fact is that we are living in an age where unity can be assured even with a decentralized pattern and with an integration in different cultures. This will be even more true of the future.

When we study, for example, the history of the Oriental schism we realize that when the Pope wrote to the Patriarch in Constantinople the letter took four months to get there. To receive a reply from the Patriarch took another four months, and because the concept of time was not the same then as now, the Patriarch probably took a month before answering. This meant an interval of nine months before communication was established, and in nine months things can change quite a bit! And maybe the Pope forgot a little bit of what he had said nine months before, and so there were all kinds of misunderstandings because of lack of communication.

But today this certainly need not be the case. For example, the Archbishop of Concepcion, in Chile, was a member of the Central Commission of the Council. In between the first two sessions he had a meeting in Rome the first week of every month, and the other three weeks of the month he was in his diocese in the very south of Chile, more than ten thousand miles from Rome. This is possible now, but was not possible even ten years ago. So you see the logic of revising our concept of unity in the Church; it is more difficult to understand when you have never taken a jet plane.

However, all these necessary adaptations called for by our meeting with the "new" continents will require on our part the attitude previously described: more one of dialogue than of immediate conversion or of imposing the Faith. And on the other hand, to establish this attitude of dialogue in the Church will mean, first of all, that many of these adaptations—liturgical, canonical, and organizational—must begin to take place in the Church.

LATIN AMERICA

We have a third area to consider in the new relations between the Church and the world: Latin America. The countries of Latin America are, culturally speaking, Catholic countries. But the fact is that in Latin America the social structure is in a state of transition from the pre-technical to the technical society, with all the consequences of which we have spoken. This change is both rapid and global, "rapid" in the sense that the process is very fast and "global" in that all institutions are affected by the change. It is not only a political change, nor an economic or educational change, but a changing of all the institutions in the society.

It is evident that the Church, too, is affected by the process of social change, and from this point of view alone she will be obliged to initiate a certain number of changes. We could almost say that the more the Church is integrated into the existing society and culture—as she is in Latin America—the more attention she will have to pay to their transformations.

If we only look at the situation as it exists at present in Latin America, we may become very pessimistic and consider the problem insoluble. And this state of mind is very bad for constructive action. We must understand that we are not confronted by a static situation but a dynamic one.

What, then, are the characteristics of the social change in Latin America? We will consider them under two aspects: the quantitative aspect and the qualitative aspect.

First, the *quantitative* aspect of social change: the demographic evolution. In 1900, the countries in this area had a population of 63 million people; in 1950, there were 153 million. In 1960, the population had risen to 220 million, and according to demographic estimates, by the year 2000 Latin America will have a population of more than 600 million people. This means that in forty years there will be an increase of more than 400 million people, more than twice the number of people who lived there during the four previous centuries from the colonial period until today!

We can already see the kind of change this is bringing about for the Church. The first consequence of the demographic evolution is the greatly increased number of inhabitants per priest: about 5,300 persons to each priest. And this ratio will not get much better in the future because of the population increase.

The parishes are also greatly affected by the increased number of people. For the entire area, the average parish has a membership of 15,332 souls and geographic dimensions of nearly 600 square miles. When we consider the great extension of the rural zones of Latin America, it is not difficult to think of immediate problems. The rural parishes, of course, always exceed the national averages, ranging from 300 square miles in the most populated areas to 1,200 square miles in the others.

However, contrary to the situation in Europe, more people live in the rural parishes of Latin America than in the urban parishes, with the exception of a certain number of big metropolitan areas. In Brazil, for example, the number of urban parishioners per parish was 11,800 in 1956 while rural parishioners numbered 14,000 per parish. In the Dominican Republic in 1960, urban parishioners were 17,600; rural, 28,400.

Parishes in the large metropolitan areas have vast numbers of parishioners. Here, for example, are some averages taken in 1960:

Rio de Janeiro	25,000	parishioners
Montevideo	25,000	"
Buenos Aires	27,000	"
Santiago	30,000	"
Mexico City	45,000	"
Havana	60,000	"

In view of these figures, then, and when we consider that the number of priests in each parish rarely reaches three, we can arrive at a more concrete and realistic concept of the pastoral burdens of the urban clergy.

Even if we can say that the large majority, over 90% as a matter of fact, of the Latin American population is baptized in the Catholic Church, it is quite obvious that most of the other sacraments are difficult, if not impossible, to receive because of the lack of priests and parochial structures.

Weekly attendance at Sunday Mass is possible only for a very small minority. In Peru and Venezuela, for example, 3%–5% of the population are the object of weekly pastoral ministry. In the cities, figures of attendance at Sunday Mass generally oscillate between 10% and 20%, and in some cases are lower than 10%. Buenos Aires, for example, has between 7% and 9% attendance at Sunday Mass.

If the attendance at Mass is not very frequent, Eucharistic participation cannot be much better. In Brazil, for example, the Eucharistic Crusade decided some time ago to discontinue their campaign for frequent communion for children, and in several areas of Colombia the clergy asks children not to receive communion on Sunday, because it would be physically impossible to distribute so many Hosts!

This non-participation in the sacraments is not, except for a fraction of the urban population, due to religious indifference, but simply to the physical impossibility of such a participation under existing conditions.

It is hardly necessary to comment on the problem of confession, or of the sacrament of the sick. These sacraments—let us state it clearly—do not exist for the majority of Latin American people.

The great increase in the number of parishioners in each parish in Latin America and the few priests available per parish has a much greater significance today, when the society is in a process of transformation, than at a time when social structures and values remained practically unchanged.

It has always been traditional in the Church to begin decentralizing pastoral structures when these failed to correspond to certain norms. When this step was not taken, a rapid movement of de-Christianization became apparent. This was the case in the European industrial milieu. Apart from the powerful ideological forces working against religion, the lack of an adaptation in pastoral approaches to the problems of the new industrial society played a decisive role in the de-Christianization of the working class.

The dynamic growth of the Church in the United States, on the other hand, can be explained by the fact that the pastoral structures kept pace admirably with the expansion of the cities, more parishes being created in the cities where the greater part of the population was concentrated.

The phenomenal increase of population in Latin America, one unparalleled in the history of humanity, demands a decentralization of pastoral structures as a first and necessary step in meeting the challenge to the Church for providing for the spiritual well-being of all her people. This conclusion is well supported by the history of the other continents.

Since we cannot foresee, at least for the next two generations, a sufficient number of priests to ensure a large-scale pastoral decentralization, and since this relatively short time-lapse will be decisive for the Latin American

Church, one conclusion becomes immediately apparent: *religious and the laity must be used in pastoral action.*

In the general panorama of the Latin American Church, women religious represent the sector of most rapid growth. Their number is increasing more rapidly than that of the population. In the four years from 1956 to 1960 the number of women religious increased by nearly 20,000 Sisters, from 80,580 to 100,200! This means that the average number of inhabitants per Sister has been lowered to about 2,003.

A great proportion of Sisters are engaged in teaching, and a large majority work in cities. Of the 7,810 religious houses of Sisters, about 500 are houses of formation and more than 3,500 are teaching. However, in many of these institutions an effort at democratization in education still remains to be realized.

The fact that the majority of the Sisters work in the cities can be explained in part by the teaching function they fulfill. It can also be explained by the almost non-existent pastoral ministry in the countryside. What superior would dare to take the responsibility of sending Sisters to places where they could go to Mass and communion only once a month or every several months?

However, it is certain (and many experiences have proved it) that the Sisters can play a very important role in the efforts for pastoral decentralization. While recognizing the aid that the Sisters can give in community development, whether in urban or rural areas, it must be pointed out that they could also contribute directly to the pastoral ministry.

They could form the catechists and control their work, prepare the people for the reception of the sacraments: baptism, confirmation, marriage, the sacrament of the sick. They could initiate the laity to certain pastoral tasks, prepare the faithful for participation in the liturgy by explaining to them the sense of the Scriptures, teaching them chant, and so on.

All this, of course, presupposes an orientation and a religious formation quite different from that which many Sisters now receive. However, this should not be too difficult to achieve, at least in some congregations which are particularly open to change. But in order to extend such pastoral action to the rural areas as well, it would be necessary to permit the Sisters to take Holy Communion themselves. Actually, this would only be an extension of a permission already in effect in some of the mission territories of Brazil.

Despite the role that can be played by the Sisters, it appears quite evident that pastoral decentralization cannot be achieved without confiding to the *laity* certain religious tasks for the service of the faithful. This applies especially to the rural communities.

The announcement of the Word of God and the task of catechesis have already been undertaken by a great number of the laity. The prayer-meetings which they direct at present could be duplicated in other places, and they could be permitted eventually to engage more widely in the distribution of certain sacraments. Then, also, why not propose the diaconate, as this seems to be the logical solution toward which we are tending?

One of the great merits of Catholic Action was the formation of laymen who are at present capable of responding worthily to such a vocation. In each diocese one could find some of these men, heads of stable families, who lead deeply religious lives. An appeal to these people would certainly not be made in vain, and, far from discouraging vocations, it would probably lead to an increase in such families as we have just mentioned.

We must realize that for the most part in Latin America when the priest is not there, the community of the faithful does not come together. Some designated leader is necessary. In other areas of the Church's missions this system of having a prayer-leader in the community is still in use, and in a successful way. This is true in the Philippines and in many countries of Africa and Asia where the vast distances and the small number of priests prevent a weekly pastoral ministry for all the faithful.

It would not be difficult to adopt a similar solution for the rural areas of Latin America, drawing on the experience of ventures already undertaken in northern Argentina or Bolivia. Ceremonies could be organized consisting of Scripture readings, psalm singing, an act of contrition, and a spiritual communion.

If ecclesiastical discipline does not stand in the way of

community prayer directed by a layman or the teaching of catechism by the laity, there are some obstacles to the distribution of certain sacraments.

At present, a layman can baptize or witness a marriage while awaiting the arrival of a priest. This authority is subject to certain dispositions according to the different localities in Latin America. However, where the community is judged to be sufficiently prepared, why not give laymen the authority to distribute Holy Communion? This has already been authorized in certain exceptional cases when the great majority of the population does not have access to the sacrament of the Eucharist.

Until now, we have been speaking about the quantitative consequences of social change in Latin America, those changes flowing from the increase in the population. We shall now consider the *qualitative* factors which depend, above all, upon the changes produced in the social life of men and their culture, that is to say, in their social *values*. These profoundly affect the life of the Church.

Latin American Catholicism has often been described as if it were only a façade or as almost exclusively superstitious. Nothing is more false. Without a doubt the forms of Catholicism which we find are still very close to a cosmic religion, where nature plays a role of prime importance, but this is very understandable when we remember that this country is just beginning to emerge from a pre-technical civilization. It is true that the evolution toward a Christianity lived in its spiritual purity and in its universal meaning is far from being accomplished. Again, mixtures exist, sometimes even downright syncretisms, as in the case of Spiritism in Brazil, or Voodoo in Haiti.

However, except for certain urban populations, it can be stated that the people of Latin America have the Faith, and that they express it in an attachment to the Church. Even in those regions abandoned by the apostolate for a long time, the response of the people to a little dynamic pastoral ministry is witness to this attachment.

How can we explain this paradox? Without rejecting supernatural explanations we must, on the other hand, take into account the natural factors involved, for these work as the normal channels of grace.

The fact of the matter is that the transmission of religious values was made, and could be made despite the lack of priests, owing to the type of society in which the great majority of the population lived—until the last few decades, the immobile society of rural areas. The immobility of this society permitted it to transmit the traditional values without difficulty. The elders exercised authority, and the patriarchal family played a basic role. Even in the absence of priests, religious values were handed down from one generation to another, not without distortions at times, but with certitude.

Furthermore, because the masses of the people were so marginal to society, they were little influenced by the anti-religious political ideas and regimes which were being developed in the cities.

Today, with more than fifty percent of the population living in an urban society, the masses are losing their two characteristics of immobility and marginality, and the social structures which until now served to transmit cultural values (among which religious values must be included), are changing radically or wholly disappearing. We can expect less and less of this sort of natural transmission of social values. Hence other, more specialized and better organized means must be developed for the transmission of religious values.

There is a danger, also, that for the Latin American masses Catholicism will become wholly identified with other cultural characteristics and will lose its spiritual significance. In other words, a person is a Catholic because he was born in such a country, in such a village, within such a family. It does not enter his mind that he could be otherwise. It would seem as abnormal for him to be a Moslem, for instance, as it seems to an Arab to be a Christian. Religion becomes more of a cultural attribute of the natural group to which he belongs and increasingly less the sign of belonging to the distinct and specific group of the Church.

In order to transmit religious values in a society where the patriarchal family no longer serves this purpose, and in a society which is becoming more pluralistic with the increase of communication, the Church must create her own instruments of transmission.

This is why there is such a great need for religious instruction and for making fullest use of the Sisters and the laity, as well as the priests, in providing for systematic action to replace the natural channels of transmission which are so rapidly changing or disappearing.

Of great importance in a dynamic apostolate is the necessity for creating a sense of belonging, a sense of Christian community, of these people in the *Church*. We spoke before of the role of the liturgical movement as a means of creating this sense of community in a society which is becoming increasingly one of secondary relationships in a mobile and urbanized world. The supernatural belonging to the Mystical Body of Christ is already achieved by baptism, of course, but this does not necessarily create the *sense* of belonging, the living *consciousness* of being a part of a social body which expresses itself visibly.

The sense of belonging is created by a real participation: in liturgical renewal, the lay apostolate, processions, and so on. We see also how the decentralization of pastoral activity plays an important role in this field.

In the transition from one type of society to another, certain fields are of key importance in the developmental process, because it is within these fields that the structures and values of the society of tomorrow are elaborated. In Latin America this is especially true of the universities, the worker movements, the nascent peasant organizations, the urban and rural co-operatives, and so on. The task of the apostolate must be undertaken, then, within these

sectors even if this means that other areas must be neglected. We must make choices, and we must base them not
on personal preferences but on factual necessities. It may
be, for example, more important to assign a priest to be
chaplain for the students in a state university than to build
a new parish.

But all this will require more than pastoral dynamism.
Social dynamism will be the sign the Church gives to men
in a developing world, just as the solicitude of Christ for
the sick and poor was the sign of His mission among the
men of His time. Men are concerned with the concrete:
they are convinced more by acts than by arguments.

In this field, the Church of Latin America has a responsibility which considerably transcends its frontiers. It is
the only large continental area which is almost homo-
geneously Catholic but where development must take
place in terms similar to those of other continents where
Christianity is a minority. Thus it will be a focal point for
these continents.

Important initiatives have already been taken in Latin
America in all these fields, and the past ten years have
marked a very decisive turning-point. Reform of the
agrarian structures, for example, has been the object of
attention of many eminent bishops. Similar determination
will also be necessary in other fields: urban, economic, and
political.

But temporal action is essentially the task of the laity.
They must receive, therefore, an orientation that will

make them conscious, as Christians, of the task to be accomplished. They must receive a formation adjusted to the needs of their time. There must be priests who accept and understand what the formation and orientation of the laity signifies in all these fields of human activity. For Christians can and must exercise a genuine social leadership in Latin America. This will be the sign of the presence of the Church in a developing world.

We can actually conclude that the Church in Latin America is faced with a missionary task: the evangelization of 400 million more people in a new society and culture which ask to be influenced and shaped by Christian values. In a relatively stable society it would be enough to exercise a ministry of preserving the faith or, if necessary, defending the faith. But we are now entering a new era, one of pastoral dynamism, which could be thought of as the second evangelization of Latin America.

THE WESTERN WORLD

The Church finds herself facing new relationships in a fourth area: the countries of the western world, especially those of Europe and North America. I will not spend much time on this point because we have gone over most of this before in our consideration of technical civilization. The fact is that it is in the western world that the Church is being confronted with all the new problems of technical society because it is in the western world that technical civilization developed and is continuing to develop more and more rapidly. And in Europe, especially, we are faced with problems which the Church has scarcely become aware of.

It has been more than ten years since real European institutions—in the sense of a community of nations—have been built up, and they have had a tremendous impact on the whole of European life. More than ten years ago tourism had become a European phenomenon with millions of people going from one country to another. With the increase in European community we have all sorts of consequences in people's lives. There is now greater freedom in the circulation of workers and of intellectuals and students from one country to another, so that mobility has vastly increased, especially for technicians.

But there are many other problems to be recognized and solutions to be undertaken. Much work remains to be done if we are to engage in a dialogue with the world of science and technology, if we are to speak the same language, to make a real contribution to these fields, to be able to meet all the problems of integrating religion in a technically developed society with all the cultural changes which have occurred, to meet the great problem of the Christianization of the working people in an industrialized society.

When we consider the experimental approaches to the question of the de-Christianization of the workers in

France, for example, we begin to realize the depth of the problem and to recognize the need for new types of action and adaptation in the Church on the pastoral level if the work of the Church is to be effectively carried out. We see that we are obliged to think these problems through. But we need not be too much discouraged at finding that there are problems to be solved; because, in a certain paradoxical way, it is the Church which thinks it has no problems whatsoever, that it has every problem solved, which is really in the worst situation, for this is the result of a certain sleepiness that comes from closing the eyes and the mind to the world we live in.

THE COMMUNIST WORLD

We come, finally, to the new relations between the Church and the communist world. I do not say new relations between the Church and communist doctrine because there is no new relation; the conflict is very clear. But between the Church and the communist world.

More than one billion people live under communist rule, and of these more than fifty-eight million are Catholics. This is almost ten percent of all the Catholics in the world.

The Church must, therefore, be concerned with this situation and must be mindful of all these people. We must follow as closely as possible what is happening in the

communist world. This is the reason why contact is necessary, so that we can know what is going on in these
countries, what the government attitudes toward the
Church and Christians are, and especially how the communist system is working and how it is evaluated. This is
very important.

We have seen in the last few years, and especially since
the time of Pope John, a change in the Church's attitude,
not toward the ideas of communism, but toward the facts
of its actual presence. This change in attitude was necessary, and is still necessary, I think, for many reasons.

First, we must know what kind of evolution is unfolding
in the communist countries. There is, of course, no change
as yet in the basic attitude of these governments, but as I
told you, there are quite a few people inside Marxism who
disagree with the official position of the party on several
questions, who think it is very out-of-date, particularly in
reference to new truths uncovered by the discoveries of
science. Already we find in the communist world some
points on which there is a whole range of differing attitudes, and even of differing opinions. This is what amazed
me so much when I went to Poland to study these problems. It was amazing to me because I had been thinking,
as I believe most of us have, of communism as something
which millions of people followed to the letter, with no
possibility of any of them having different opinions.

Perhaps Poland was not the best country on which to
base an optimistic judgment, because a great deal more

liberalism has been permitted in Poland than in the other communist countries, like Hungary and even Russia itself. But it is an important fact that already we find within Marxism quite a few different directions of thought.

The second reason for maintaining contacts with the communist world is that there is a great social evolution going on inside communism due to the very factors I told you about in the development of technical civilization. This development brings with it many new problems, maybe even more problems to the communist world than to other countries.

Now that the standard of living is rising, now that in many of the communist countries the fundamental needs of life are being met by social and economic organizations, there is developing, as a consequence, a greater desire for freedom from the social and intellectual point of view. And so, even now, without a word said and without any official change in the doctrine, a greater liberalization of the system is under way.

The evolution of technical civilization does not present the Christian world with problems which affect basic doctrines of the Church, because Christianity is transcendent, it extends beyond this world. But technical civilization does present communism with serious *problems of doctrine* because their doctrine is based upon a specific interpretation of the world and a particular situation of mankind, on an interpretation made at a certain stage in the evolution of man. Now that the continuing process of man's evolution has so considerably altered these basic factors, the communist doctrine will require more and more *essential* changes, especially from the practical point of view. On the other hand, when we speak of change in the Church in face of the problems of technical civilization, we do not refer to any change in the *content,* in the doctrines of the Church, but changes in the *ways* in which this is brought to men who live in different ages.

When we analyze from a purely technical standpoint, without any reference to philosophical ideals, what communism has been to technical civilization, we can see that it has played much the same role in one part of the world in the change from the pre-technical, rural type of society to the technical, urban society as capitalism played for another part of the world. But both systems have evolved with one or another form of human exploitation.

Today the countries behind the Iron Curtain are developing in such a way that in the future, even if they keep their doctrine, their ideology, and their philosophy, a much more liberal system may prevail, even in Russia. In the long run this cannot fail to be the case because the cultural aspirations at work in the people will make it impossible to preserve for long the rigid system which has been in force during their transition from a rural to a technical society. We must examine the facts very closely, and I think we shall find that this situation is not without an historical parallel.

The French Revolution, for example, was, in addition to attempting the establishment of an "ideal" society, very much involved with the complex changes which accompanied the transition from a rural to an industrialized society. In a way, that industrial society could not have developed without something like the revolutions in Europe. It is not necessary that this change be accomplished by a bloody revolution, but some kind of revolution, bloody or peaceful, is necessary to bring about needed land reform in the average pre-technical society, to change the social structure, and to enable a middle class to develop. (It is this very situation now in Latin America—the emergence from a rural to a technical civilization—that is calling forth all our efforts to keep the change a peaceful one. So far, our efforts have not matched the urgency which the situation demands.)

At first the French Revolution was tremendously anti-clerical and anti-religious, even more so, perhaps, than communism has been. Twenty-five years later Napoleon had negotiated a concordat with the Church and the Faith emerged stronger than before.

We must be realists, and much as we would wish it otherwise, realize that in this age far more time and effort will be needed before a solution is reached. But we may hope that much will be done toward settling the problems that can be settled, toward reaching some practical meas-

ures of co-existence and some kind of co-operation where-
ever this proves possible.

I was quite impressed by a group of young Catholic
adults when I was in Poland. We had several meetings
and discussions about the position of Christians in the
socialist-communist countries. As Catholics, they were
very much discouraged by the idea of supporting an
entirely negative position in reference to the society in
which they lived.

In substance, what they said was: "We have been told
only and always to be negative, negative, negative about
everything, because we live in a communist regime. Every
change in society, every change in the economy, everything that is happening in our country is *a priori* barred
to us—because we are in a communist country. We are
not in agreement with the communist ideology, but we
can see some positive aspects to the type of society in
which we are living, even some cases where conditions are
better here than in the free world—the urban situation,
for instance. We would like to be able to participate in
some of these things, because if we keep aloof from all
participation in our society, we leave the field completely
free for the communists. One day we hope the Church
will be able to resume her evangelical mission in the
socialist world. That day may already be at hand. But if
we who live in these countries are not preparing for this
day, who will be the missionaries in the socialist world?"
This was, I thought, an interesting observation.

These people were not collaborating at all with the communist party. But there are some Catholic groups in these countries who are collaborating with the communists even from the ideological point of view. The "Pax" group in Poland is perhaps the most widely known example. This originated as a "Catholic" group, which set forth the idea that despite a disagreement of viewpoint, Catholics could support socialist progress in a communist state. After the 1956 revolt in Poland this group (whose leaders had been pro-fascist before the war) still continued to support the Stalinist line. They were, of course, openly denounced by Cardinal Wyszynski.

So, as I have said before, we cannot be over-simplistic in our approach to these problems. Nor should we be so naive as to think that communism will automatically fall apart at our feet when ideological cracks appear in its doctrinal foundation. Communism is still very strong, and it may be that we will yet have more persecution from it. We must realize, too, that the dialogue which now exists in Poland between the Catholics and some of the Marxists is altogether impossible in Cuba, because Cuba is still in the first stage of communism.

During my visit to Cuba in June of 1963, I attended several meetings with Catholic lay people and priests. In private some of them asked me if I thought the time had come to begin a dialogue with the Cuban regime. I suppose they may have been encouraged by the fact that, as I told you, the Cuban government allowed 10,000 copies of Pope John's encyclical to be published, and thought that the time had come to press for further progress. But, trying to give good advice, I said I thought that at that time it would be impossible, that the best thing to do was to be quiet and wait: later perhaps it would be possible.

Thoughts of these kinds seem to bring great confusion to the minds of many people. Sometimes you wonder whether you should bring such matters up at all, but I repeat: we cannot allow ourselves to be too simplistic about complex problems. Often we reach in such an emotional way to the problem of communism that there seems an automatic absence of rationality in our attitudes.

5 New Organizations in the Church

Many aspects of the world today call for new organizations in the Church if she is faithfully to carry out her mission in an increasingly complex society.

NATIONAL CONFERENCES OF BISHOPS

When the First Vatican Council began about one hundred years ago, in 1869 to be exact, there were about 600 bishops in the world; today there are about 3,000. This fact alone argues the necessity for some new type of organization, for some new type of organized relationship between the Pope and the bishops. It is not particularly feasible to run an organization directed by a Board of 3,000 members in the same way that an institution with a Board of 600 can be run. And there are only 365 days in the year. It is really impossible now for the Pope to meet each of 3,000 bishops personally and to be kept informed directly by each bishop each year on conditions in each particular diocese. It is not difficult to imagine how involved this situation would become.

Of course that is why, in the more primitive days of the Church's organization, the Curia came very rapidly to be of such importance as the intermediary between the Pope and the ever-growing number of bishops. This is a sociological fact showing how a practical solution arose to meet the lag between the growth of the Church and the adaptation of her organizational structures. Now this empirical approach to the problem has to be countered by a theological approach. We must correct the too great power acquired by bureaucracy with a more collegial organization of authority in the Church.

Every year between 50 and 75 new dioceses are created in the Church. Within eight years the Papal Nuncio to Brazil, Bishop Lombardi, created 73 new dioceses in Brazil alone!

All these new dioceses mean that the number of auxiliary bishops must be increased too, and this calls for greater organization. This is why, shortly after the First World War, the American bishops drew up the constitution of the National Conference of American Bishops. This constitution, drawn up in 1919, was not authorized by the Holy See until 1922. Fear of Gallicanism and of nationalism delayed recognition.

And that is the reason why the bishops' conference of America is called the National Catholic Welfare Conference. Of course, it *was* organized for national welfare. It began in 1917, actually, as the National Catholic War

Conference, to co-ordinate and carry out the welfare activities of the bishops of the United States during the First World War. After the war it was reorganized as the National Catholic Welfare Conference, which simply continued the bishops' organization without even changing the name very much. This conference has become the real organ of the American hierarchy, but it has never been given a proper name. It is rather unusual for a bishops' conference to be called a national welfare conference. Of course most people call it the NCWC and many of them don't know what the letters stand for!

But since that time, and especially since World War II, these bishops' conferences have been really encouraged by the Holy See: we are coming to recognize the need for such organizations to act as intermediary bodies between the Holy See, the Pope, and individual bishops. Although each bishop has the right to go directly to the Pope, it is not really possible or necessary to do so except in most unusual circumstances. For the normal problems of the Church and for the normal needs of administration, we will come to rely more upon the national conferences.

CENTRALIZATION AND DECENTRALIZATION

The possibilities of communication in the world today permit a greater decentralization in the powers of decision with far less danger than ever before to the unity of the

Church. It would be quite possible now to have meetings of all the presidents or delegates of the national bishops' conferences about twice a year in Rome.

It would be possible to have several mobile Papal delegates, who would be in contact with whole continents, or specialists in certain fields who would travel, meeting with responsible people in the different countries. They could go back and forth to Rome very easily and quickly.

Intercultural meetings, with people from Europe coming to the United States and speaking here, and people from America addressing groups in Europe and elsewhere —this exchange is very conducive to unity.

The tremendous power of the mass media for unity cannot be underestimated. The person of the Pope has become a symbol of the unity of the Church, and the press, radio, and television make his presence a direct experience for millions of people. Through the mass media his words can be carried to every part of the world. This is a great force for unity.

All these opportunities for assuring the unity of the Church have contributed to the development of ideas for the decentralization of some powers within the Church. The idea of establishing the national bishops' conferences and of granting the bishops' conferences real powers of decision in liturgical and ecclesiastical fields is being seriously considered; the question of the re-establishment of the diaconate in certain countries, with married or unmarried deacons performing some sacramental functions on the approval of the bishops' conferences in those countries, is being considered. This would mean that the national conferences would have real powers of decision over many matters of particular importance in their own national situation.

NEW INTERMEDIARY BODIES

At the same time that we are considering the decentralization of some powers within the Church, we must recognize the necessity for more centralized, more co-ordinated types of action. And this will result in new institutions.

Our present diocesan system, in which the bishop is almost all-powerful, is not wholly adapted to the work of the Church today. There is a real necessity not only for some kind of decentralization of the Church's central organization, but also for some kind of centralization in the feudal type of organization within the dioceses. It is very difficult to achieve any collective action on a national level because thus far the national conferences of bishops which do exist have no real authority, serving chiefly as a vehicle for furthering mutual acquaintance and co-ordinating certain kinds of activities. But where there is not unanimity, there is no way of inducing a bishop to comply with a decision of the other bishops of the conference.

Many, many times very small minorities—even a minority of one bishop, for example, in small countries—can prevent all kinds of decisions which are of urgent necessity for the Church in her mission. There are so many new aspects of the apostolate that these simply must be organized on a national level.

So the establishment of the national bishops' conferences with actual powers of decision would serve a dual intermediary role: (1) that of contributing to a decentralization of the Church's authority by giving the conferences power to resolve certain questions of national administrative need and indigenous problems, and (2) that of centralizing the authority of the bishops of the nation as a body in view of common decisions binding on all dioceses.

New intermediary organizations are not only needed for the episcopate; there are many other areas where common decisions of some sort need to be made. We find a recognition of this need in the Conferences of Major Superiors for the Religious. And the same thing is happening on another level for pastoral work, not yet in the United States to any great extent, but more often in Europe and Latin America.

We call this movement Integrated Pastoral Action, or pastoral planning for a whole city, a whole diocese, or a whole nation. We are in the process of forming new institutions for this work. I was at a meeting in Montreal recently at which integrated pastoral work for the whole diocese of Montreal was under discussion. Many new types of organization are involved. First, there must be a center of responsibility for pastoral co-ordination for the whole city. Then pastoral counselors must be appointed for all the sectors of the apostolate. Finally a secretariat is required. As a result, all kinds of new organizations are developing.

We have not heard very much about "deans" in the Church in the United States, but this office is becoming of great importance in Latin America and in European countries, especially France. Perhaps this is a result of the decentralization of the diocese, and each dean has the responsibility of ten to fifteen parishes. At first this was more of an administrative position, but now it is oriented from the pastoral point of view and the dean is responsible for the pastoral work of these parishes. So we are coming to new definitions of the functions of the dean and also to new geographical definitions of the deaneries, in order to produce greater homogeneity from a sociological standpoint. This will make it easier for the deans to work together, meet together, and make some decisions together, and will thus enable them to be a liaison between the individual priests and the bishop for pastoral work. This is on a smaller scale than the bishops' conferences but based on a similar approach.

All these new kinds of responsibilities, these intermedi-

ary bodies which are being created in the organization
of the Church, are really necessary, for they are, in a
paradoxical sense, the pivots for decentralization on the
one hand and for a needed form of centralization on the
other.

6 *New Types of Action*

With the increase of new organizations we see also *new types of action.* The specialized institutions of technical civilization which have replaced the polyvalent institutions have developed also in the pastoral activity of the Church.

SPECIALIZED INSTITUTIONS

We spoke of the fact that the technical society requires more specialized institutions in the fields of economy, leisure, education, and so on, and that these institutions have a monovalent type of responsibility. In other words, if we have a factory producing shoes—well, then it will not be producing bicycles. Or in the field of leisure, if we have a sports club, it will not be engaged in producing motion pictures.

This type of specialized activity is arising very rapidly in the Church, in every diocese, in every nation, to meet the special religious needs of the apostolate.

Liturgical centers are an example. The liturgy was and is a matter for the parish. But because of the renewal of emphasis on the liturgy, the advance in liturgical thought, the number of new records and books and theological studies, there is a need for *specialists* aware of all these developments and for instruments for their diffusion. It is too much to expect every priest, Sister and layman to keep abreast of this movement all over the world, and so we have seen the birth of many kinds of liturgical institutions.

The same thing is true of the formation of the laity for greater participation in the liturgy. We need people to serve as lay lectors to read the Epistles and Gospels in the vernacular, and for this they must have some training. Instead of having each parish undertake this training, institutes or classes in adult education are being organized in many cities, to which parishes can send people for a few weeks of special courses.

Catechetical centers also are being formed in all countries in order to keep up with innovations in catechetical teaching which are arising from this process of adaptation to the age we are living in. These train lay teachers and distribute information on new advances in this specialized field.

Another very well-organized activity, especially in some cities, is the *Cana Conference movement,* a specialized institution for the preparation of young couples about to be married (Pre-Cana) and for the continued formation of married couples (Cana).

All these institutions are performing functions which were previously carried on by the parish as a polyvalent institution or simply not performed at all because the need for them was nonexistent. But in our technical world, in our socialized type of civilization, we have seen in the Church during the last fifty years the growth of a great number of specialized types of religious activity, of religious groups, and of religious movements. So, the integration of a Christian in the Church today is made not only on the parish level but also through participation in several other specialized religious institutions and groups on a non-parochial level.

In discussing the work of the specialized institutions we might seem to imply that parochial organizations no longer exist. But they do, and in great numbers. This is not so much of a problem in the United States, and I can remember that when I first came here and lived in a parish in Chicago I was simply amazed at how few parochial organizations the American parishes had in comparison with urban European parishes. In our urban European parishes, and in French Canadian parishes, it is quite common to have between fifty and sixty parish organizations! Of course it is impossible to go on like that, impossible for the priests to have time to attend to all these things. So we must find out what organizations are really worth keeping and which should be discontinued.

From another point of view, it is necessary to see if

there is any alternative to the actual presence of a priest at all the meetings. In Guatemala, for example, where there are very few priests, the national chaplain for the Young Christian Workers is also pastor of one of the largest parishes. At the same time he is acting as chancellor for the diocese, and since there are no other YCW chaplains in his city, he is chaplain for the city also. It is impossible for him, if this organization is to operate not only in the city but throughout the country, to be present at every meeting. So once a month he meets with the leaders of each section and goes over the program for the month, instructing them on how to carry it out, and they then give the religious formation themselves.

There is no reason why only priests should be able to do this. Sisters can do the same thing, and so can the laity. The fact that we all have so little time is perhaps partly due to poor organization. We must revise our ideas on the kind of organizations most needed for the Church and also on when our personal participation is really necessary.

DEVELOPMENT OF SERVICES

In the evolution of urban society, as we have seen, there has come about a great increase in the number of services available to people and a new type of social relationship between those offering the service and those accepting it which is not based on a person-to-person knowledge of each other and not especially intended to result in this primary type of relationship. These "secondary-relationship" services are becoming very important, too, in the work of the Church.

For example, in a city like Chicago, one married couple, one priest and one doctor, speaking ten or fifteen times a year to as many as a thousand young couples, helping them to prepare for marriage, are performing an extraordinary type of apostolate. Their work can have a lasting effect on the marriages and family lives of all these people. And this does not mean that the doctor, the priest and the married couple need keep up personal relations with everyone in the audience. It would be impossible—they would have no time left to do their own work.

Of course some very difficult problems require personal contact. But rather than try to solve each individual problem put before them, they can give as great service by referring these people to some other priest, doctor or marriage counselor for individual help.

The study-weeks and workshops sponsored by organizations like the Sister Formation Conference, or YCS, YCW, CFM and others, all utilize and benefit from the secondary relationships on which they are established.

Another kind of work very important in the modern world is that carried on through the mass media. (If Bishop Sheen had had to become personally acquainted with all the people who have watched him on television,

I don't think he would still be among the living!) But this kind of work, contact through mass media—through newspapers, magazines, books, the telephone—is all of great importance.

In quite a few cities in Europe telephone services have been set up where you can ask any kind of question of a religious or moral nature and find someone to help you, any time from 6 A.M. to midnight. This service was begun three or four years ago. In Brussels we now have three lines functioning almost all day, and we have also organized a whole referral system with doctors, priests, lawyers, psychiatrists, and so on, who have agreed to take calls involving their specialty. This is a typical service, and the anonymity is one reason for its great success. If a question is too complicated, the inquirer is asked to call back after a certain period when, if possible, someone will have an answer. Sometimes people who were about to commit suicide have been kept talking till a priest could get to them. So this is a quite wonderful form of verbal apostolate.

The question of spiritual direction, which used to be an almost exclusively individualistic kind of activity, is being viewed somewhat differently today. We are coming to a more collective type of spiritual direction. For example, the new Family movements in France are emphasizing a more definite spiritual development. The fact that these people meet every month to discuss their problems—of prayer, spiritual life, Christian attitudes, married life—makes them need much less individual spiritual direction than before. Most of their problems are now examined and resolved in a "team" situation.

Of course individual spiritual direction is still needed for some problems, but this great movement of teams among Christians is accomplishing much of what was formerly provided by individual direction. The same thing is true for priests. More and more we are forming teams of priests, meeting together monthly and making what we call a "revision of life" very similar to that practiced by Catholic Action groups. We do this to help ourselves in our priestly life, to discuss together all the problems we encounter in the apostolate and in our own prayer life.

This is the kind of teamwork in the spiritual field that reduces the importance of individual spiritual directors. We are of course happy that there is an increase of religious consciousness among Catholics, but it would be impossible to give each one personal spiritual direction every two weeks. It is a big problem for priests, and quite a decision to make, whether they should go on accepting all the requests they get for personal advice and spiritual direction, or consecrate more time to collective direction. When a priest finds that he is spending so much time giving individual direction that he cannot get his other work done, there is a serious conflict for him to resolve.

In the most advanced seminaries the whole organization is based on teams. Each team has the technical assistance of one of the priests, but they themselves have a great responsibility for each seminarian. I know of one seminary which has had this system in effect for about ten years with really extraordinary success. The team may even make a judgment on the vocations of the seminarians. They take their work very seriously, and it is making a great contribution to the deepening of their spiritual life.

To take another example. There is much work to be done among students in universities and colleges, especially in non-Catholic universities. This is true of North America as it is of all countries, but it is absolutely essential that it should be done in Latin America. We must realize that there are thousands of Catholic students attending non-Catholic universities, and that with the exception of one or two countries in the world, we will never be able to establish Catholic universities to educate all our young Catholic men and women.

In Latin America the university has an added significance. As in most underdeveloped countries it is, for the present, the main channel for social mobility, for social ascension. Having a university degree gives one prestige, and in a closed society with a small group of people monopolizing all the power—political, cultural, economic and social—one of the few, if not the only, means of participation, of breaking through the barrier, is the university. This is why it is so important in Latin America. And eighty-five percent of the students are in non-Catholic universities! If we concentrate all our efforts on Catholic universities, we can see what will happen.

In the United States Newman Clubs are very active at many secular universities, and they have gained in importance in the past few years; but they are all directed by priests. Why not think of work in this line for Sisters? It could be a very important field for them, but they must be well prepared before undertaking this apostolate, for two reasons.

In the first place, they must be Sisters who are specially suited to work with students, not only Catholic students but students as a whole in secular universities. Students have psychological characteristics which make them difficult to reach, and the religious chosen for participation in this kind of work must be very carefully selected. It would seem that the very first requirement for a Sister in this field should be a university degree, and if at all possible, one from a secular university. This is to assure her position as a woman, rather than as a religious. Her social status must be built up on the fact that she is one of the group, an equal, one who has lived through the experience of an education in the university—not as a matter of pride, but as a basis for mutual respect and understanding.

This background is necessary for acceptance, for the right to speak and be listened to not just because she is a religious but as an educated person. This is only the first requirement, but I think it is essential. All the other personal characteristics and attitudes needed for work with young adults must also be present, but her relationship with the students must be rooted in respect and admiration for intellectual attainments as well as affection and respect for personal holiness.

We must be prudent for a second reason. In Europe and in the countries of Latin America it is very difficult for Sisters to gain acceptance in this type of work. In Europe especially, the religious vocation is held in low esteem because of the impression that Sisters are very marginal to society. This is why the secular institutes in Europe are gaining so much support and are undertaking more and more of this type of work with university students in Paris, Rome and other cities.

But there is a great need for qualified Sisters in this field.

THE LAY APOSTOLATE

We have been living in a time when most of the functions in the Church have been monopolized by what we could call a "clerical class." There have been many reasons for this, but the result has been that formal leadership in the Church has been almost completely absorbed by the clergy, to such an extent that when we speak of "leadership" in the Church, the term is synonymous with "clergy." And although in the past few decades we have seen the development of more intellectual and other activity in the "lay" apostolate, this has been thought of largely in terms of "free-time" activity, rather than as the development of roles of responsible leadership in the work of the Church. Some of our best lay people today are discouraged by the many difficulties they encounter in trying to understand what they could or what they should do in order to contribute their talents effectively to the apostolate.

Much of the difficulty arises from a lack of thought concerning the respective roles of the laity and the clergy. You have heard, for example, that the priest should concern himself only with spiritual things, and the next thing you know he is becoming active in fields which are "proper" to the laity: social justice, business ethics, labor organizations, race relations. And you have heard similar remarks made concerning the "intrusion" of the laity into fields which are the concern of the clergy: catechetical work, teaching religion or theology, participation in diocesan advisory commissions, marriage preparation and counseling, and so on. I really think that if we go on like this, splitting hairs, we shall never solve this problem. Some really constructive thought must be given to a theology of the laity and a theology of the clergy.

But because of vital, existential experiences we can see more clearly how these new functions are developing. And we are coming to very new developments in the Church. So in Latin America the new roles and functions of the lay people in the Church will, because we are living through these experimental years, help us to define more clearly the role of the laity in the Church and the real distinction between religious status, clerical status, and lay status in the apostolate.

The Christian presence in the world today is much more complex because we are living in a much more complex civilization than those of the past. When the industrial world was coming into being, it soon became clear that priests and Sisters could not have a monopoly of the apostolate simply because they were not present in many spheres of this new society. This was one of the beginnings of awareness of the whole problem.

But much thinking remains to be done.

NEW DIMENSIONS: LITURGICAL AND CATECHETICAL

All the changes in the world, both in the technically developed countries and in those now developing, are bringing about new ways of viewing many activities which have existed since the beginning of the Church, really, but are being seen in entirely new dimensions in the light of present-day developments.

We have already pointed out the importance of the *liturgical renewal* in an urban, mobile civilization as an expression of Christian community, and how liturgical life has been greatly re-emphasized in its original social aspect.

Catechetical work has undergone a tremendous renewal. It has acquired a new dimension for the transmission of religious values in a technical civilization. This activity has always been performed, of course, in all societies, but with the great changes now coming about in the cultures of the underdeveloped countries and the consequences of a mobile society, religious values are not being automatically transmitted from one generation to another as they were in a rural, pre-technical civilization. So catechetical work has become very important as the means for transmitting the Faith, and must now, more than ever, be seen as extending to adults and not just to children.

The development of *ecumenism* is also related to the growth of a technical civilization. We haven't time to treat this important field fully, but I would like to point out that the material background of ecumenism is very closely related to the increase of means of communication. It is not surprising that this great movement had its origin after the First Wold War and has developed especially since the Second World War.

We have had much more contact with other religious groups and have faced the necessity for meeting with them, especially in reference to missionary activity. We have spoken of the aggressive action of Colombian Catholics toward some Protestant groups in Colombia and vice versa, and of the fact that we must realize that, because of world-wide communications, what might be a local situation becomes magnified in the eyes of the world and is made symbolic. This is why we must learn to see our actions in a global vision, as they affect others throughout the world.

We have seen, too, a great new emphasis placed upon *biblical studies* and scholarship, with new light being shed upon traditional biblical interpretations, new discoveries, and new insights gained from our vantage point in history.

There are, then, many new dimensions of action and renewal in the Church today that have come about because of the changes in our world. It is true that if we look upon the growth and development of human civilization as accidental and material progress as a necessary evil, it will give scandal to say that all these renewals in the Church have been produced by the changes in our civilization. But if we take a true spiritual attitude in viewing the world and material progress—seeing the role of providence in shaping the Church and the world in accordance with God's plan for men—then it is not in the least scandalous to say that these changes have come about as the result of developments in the world, because we believe that God speaks to us not only through Revelation and tradition but in the unfolding facts of the world we now live in. That is why we can say that owing to technological developments we are, for example, able to discover new and different aspects of Christ's message, to develop many more aspects of theology, of the liturgy, and of many other kinds of action in the Church.

7 *New Roles*

The new relations between the Church and the world, the new organizations, the new institutions, and the new dimensions of action have brought about *new roles* in the Church today.

NEW ROLES FOR THE CLERGY

We have already mentioned quite a few new roles in the discussion of the new organization. For example, when we have a bishops' conference established there must be a president, a secretary, and perhaps a treasurer, too. These are new roles to be filled. When we change our deaneries from administrative jurisdictions to pastoral jurisdictions, this again creates new roles.

We are in the same situation in many other fields. For example, there are a few priests like myself who are attached to a diocese but working on a national or an international level. In some respects, you know, this situation is not exactly normal, or at least it has not yet been normal-ized. But it should be, because each diocese has to recognize that it has a universal aspect. We must re-examine the role of the bishop, rediscover the universal responsibility, the collective responsibility for the universal Church, as the first responsibility of the bishop. And his secondary responsibility is to his diocese, because of the existential fact that the work of the Church has to be divided into parts, and a particular responsibility for one part given to each bishop as his share in it.

All these roles have to be re-examined and redivided progressively but not too rapidly; otherwise we shall institutionalize some situations before they have evolved to maturity.

NEW ROLES FOR SISTERS

New roles are opening up, too, for the religious, for Sisters. I should probably have taken up the subject of the emancipation of women, which is another aspect of technical civilization, and one which has been very well covered in the second chapter of Cardinal Suenens' book *The Nun in the World*. But the result of this emancipation is that women in all capacities receive more and more responsibility, and more and more equality with men, not only as to job opportunities or wages (although there is still some inequality here), but also as to leadership and intellectual undertakings. This is, of course, having a great impact on the Church. And in a sense we in the Church are being very, very slow to recognize this development and adapt ourselves to it.

Just one indication of this is the fact that not even one woman was involved in the preparations for the Council. I don't say to speak in the Council (it is perhaps too early to hope for that)—but at least some women could have been appointed to commissions preparing for the Council. We have one million religious, and so far as I know—if my statistics are right—about half the Church is made up of women, and maybe even a little more! So we still have a need for adaptation in the Church along these lines.

There are great problems in religious congregations, especially in Europe, because of the lack of adaptation to modern times in religious life as a whole. And if this problem is, at the moment, particularly acute in Europe, I am very much concerned that the same trend could occur here in the United States. The fact that the religious roles of priest and Sister are very highly esteemed in the United States right now can work in an ambivalent way simply because it can lead to complacency and blindness to the necessity for some adaptation in the religious life and in Church organization until it is too late.

In Europe, however, the fact is that the status of the woman religious in society is very low. And this is surely one of the main reasons for the great and very rapid diminution of vocations among the congregations of European Sisters. Another is the fact that the new roles and new responsibilities opened to the Sisters were not taken up by them. In those congregations that are rapidly adapting themselves to the new opportunities, we find an immediate rise in vocations. This is also, I suppose, why the increase of secular institutes has been so rapid in Europe: something new was necessary because of the lack of adaptation.

Until just a short time ago women in Europe, including Sisters, were not permitted to take a doctorate in theology. I met a very interesting woman working as a lay apostle in Jamaica who was a doctor of theology, but she had received her doctorate from a Protestant faculty because it was not possible to take it in a Catholic university. This was in Germany. And at Louvain University women are still not allowed, at least according to the rules, to teach as full-time professors. There are perhaps two women teaching there now, so we are making some progress, but you can see that we are in pretty bad shape from this point of view. In the United States, fortunately, women do not have this problem to such an extent.

When we hear about religious statistics in Latin America—comparisons between the formal Church leadership in Latin American countries and the number of Catholics these leaders are responsible for—we think only in terms of the number of *priests*. We say that there are 5,300 Catholics for every priest in Latin America, and when we compare this with Protestant missions, we say that there are 300 to 400 Protestants to every minister. But the Protestants include in their statistics women as well as men working in the mission field, and we never think to mention 100,000 religious when we make the comparison! This is just another indication of our tendency to think of leadership as being identified with the clergy.

You can see why we are under the necessity of thinking about and creating many new roles and responsibilities for religious in the mission of the Church. I will give you a few examples that come to mind; undoubtedly there are many others.

A field that is very undeveloped in the Church, where Sisters could be of tremendous help and influence, is that of *religious statistics*. Such statistics about the Church and her activity are very necessary in the modern world as an instrument of self-knowledge, in order to judge our action. When we take a look at the only statistics that are published in the Pontifical Yearbook, it is almost unbelievable to see how little we know about our actions. And when we think of the scope of the Church's activity in the world today, it is almost inconceivable that we can seriously undertake this work without at least a minimum of good statistics.

One congregation of Sisters, the Missionaries of Jesus Crucified, in Brazil, has seen the need for this very clearly, and a team of fifteen of them is doing outstanding work in religious statistics, working especially in the social field, as is their entire congregation. The order has become a very dynamic one, having grown to almost 2,500 members in just a few years. This team of Sisters is organizing statistics on religious congregations—how many men? how many women? the type of work done? the number of schools, pupils, hospitals? social work? and so on. And their work is providing the Nuncio with a very valuable instrument for defining new dioceses in Brazil. That is why Bishop Lombardi is able to make more meaningful decisions concerning the establishment of new dioceses than perhaps any other Nuncio, at least in Latin America. Because he has all the data. You might almost say that the Sisters are defining the dioceses in Brazil, because they say, in effect, to the Nuncio: If you want to make a a new diocese in this area, the boundaries should be thus and so, because of the geography, because of the social distribution of the population, because this is the number of priests, of Sisters, of schools you will have there, and so on.

The same thing happens when new congregations of Sisters want to work in Brazil. They go there and say, for example, that they are able to staff a vocational school, where should they be? And at once these Sisters would be able to say: We need a vocational school here or there or somewhere else—take your choice. This is a real instrument for the Church. It is needed in all countries, but the need is not yet very much understood. This congregation began in a very modest way, but they now have Sisters who have graduated in statistics. And they are becoming more highly educated all the time. The superior of these Sisters, who was once the provincial, told me that she had never felt so apostolic in her life as since she has been working on these statistics because she saw the great value to the action of the Church in this instrument. Well, in Belgium, I've been looking for about six years for a congregation of Sisters who understand this, and I haven't found them yet. I have almost reached the point of asking the Sisters from Brazil to come and organize the religious statistics of Belgium.*

Another field is *sociological research,* not only research in the sociology of religion but knowledge in the sociological field to help us to understand all the changes taking place in society and all the consequences for the Church. We need Sisters able to think in a prospective way about changes in society and how these will affect the organization of the Church, and the action of the Church, a few years from now. They must think about the consequences of these changes and the effect they will have on their role, in the field of education, say, or in hospitals.

In one country I have been trying to persuade the Sisters to get together some statistics about the various religious congregations. I haven't succeeded, and I know why. Because they don't dare. They are afraid to see what the actual conditions are in these congregations. Well, if we don't dare to look now, the day will come in five, ten, or twenty years when decisions will have to be made, and made very rapidly, about things we could be thinking about right now and making plans for.

* Since these lectures were given a congregation has been founded.

Many religious will die in the course of the next ten years, and we are not getting the same rate of replacement. This means that we shall have to abandon some tasks or make drastic changes, and if we do not study the problems now, we shall not be prepared to make them. If changes are not considered, they will not be forthcoming. Many Sisters will be so overworked by that time that more of them will die, and others become mentally or physically ill. Of course by then everyone will agree that we should think of reorganization, adaptation, and all the rest—things we could and should be considering now. But we need instruments: we need statistics, we need sociological knowledge, we need people trained in these fields.

The same holds true for priests in dioceses where vocations are decreasing or where it is necessary to send priests to other countries, like those of Latin America. There must be some thought given to diocesan reorganization and adaptation. And this thought is necessary not only for the organization of the Church, but also for the mission of the Church.

Therefore we need trained people. And it will be too late to begin to form, say, Sisters in these fields at the time when we are really feeling the necessity for this in a vital way. It takes four or five years just for the training, and another five years for enough practice and experience to have a person fully formed in these areas. If we do not begin now, we will not have those people prepared in ten years, when the great part of the Church will become aware of how badly they are needed.

We need people specially trained in *psychology* and *biology*, not just capable of teaching these as subjects but capable of reflection, of creative thought in these fields. We are very late, as we said before, in our thinking about the new discoveries of science in biology and psychology, in problems such as birth control, life processes, personality changes, emotional disorders, and the rest. But with some people—priests, Sisters, and laymen—trained in these areas we would be better able to keep our theological thought abreast of new developments, and this would be of immense value to the Church. We are in a world which is in a state of perpetual mutation, and there must be a corresponding rapidity in our answers to the questions which are constantly arising.

We see the possibilities, then, for many new roles. Therefore we need among Sisters (and I say "Sisters" because they are the great "manpower" reserve in the Church) those who are able to meet the world on its own level. I don't say that we must abandon the teaching of children—it is neither necessary nor desirable to have 80,000 Sisters in North America in more highly specialized work—but it is very important for the social acceptance of Sisters in a technical civilization that they be recognized as competent in all fields which are open to women in general. If we limit the image of Sisters to women in the classroom—be it grammar school, high school, or even the colleges—but as not able to go farther or more extensively into wider fields of activity, we shall not be able to meet the world on these levels.

We must assure the presence of Sisters in society; we must form Sisters as really active members of society and at all levels—not just confined to their work in hospitals or in the schools, but participating in the neighborhood councils, and in all kinds of activities which are taking place in the community at the level at which they are working. This is very important for their status and one of the best means of avoiding an image of Sisters, like the one in Europe, as completely marginal to society.

With regard to the new roles of which we have spoken, many of which require professional training, we must always remember that if professional training is needed, it must be undertaken in the spirit of the apostolate. It must not be undergone just for the pleasure of being a professional, not just because of the necessity for doing a secular task, but for the sake of the mission of the Church in the world.

We must be efficient, also, in that we must make a choice among the tasks and professions in which Sisters are to be oriented. For the good of the universal Church in a given society we may have to slow down some types of activity we are now engaged in and enter others. But in making these choices we must keep in mind that *the main purpose of the Christian community in the world is to as-*

sure the presence of Christ in the world, to bear witness to
His redeeming love for all men.

Finally, let us realize that the assumption of these new
roles, these new responsibilities, these new opportunities,
will have quite a few consequences in the life of congregations, and for Sisters. Many of these new roles and tasks
will not be performed by every congregation because they
are so specialized.

Until now, whenever a new need has arisen in the
Church, one of the traditional answers has been the creation of a new congregation. When there was a need for
the redemption of prisoners from Islam a congregation,
the Croisiers, was formed for this purpose. In the nineteenth century, because education was becoming a social
value desired by everyone, we saw the establishment of
many congregations for this purpose. At that time society
was moving toward a democratization of education, so
this service was a real testimony of charity in those days.

Now that we are coming to a time where education has
become a social right—recognized by society, by the state,
by law—the sense of the testimony has changed. Educational work and the role of the Sisters who perform it are
no longer seen by society as a testimony of charity, but
only as a job to be done.

This fact should cause us to re-evaluate our presence in
these fields. Not that educational tasks cannot be performed with charity or that personal testimony cannot be
given through them, but the testimony of collective char-

ity may have disappeared from some types of education and some types of hospital care, because these fields have become recognized responsibilities of society.

So the collective meaning of these tasks has completely changed in a modern society, and Catholic education, for example, is more and more seen, not as a service to man in a growing culture, but as a service to the "ghetto" Catholic community. We must learn to look at our collective tasks in the Church with awareness of the changes in their collective meaning.

As we have noted, many of these new tasks will not be performed by every congregation, and we are no longer in an age when a new congregation is created for each new task. We must come to collective work. In several centers for socio-religious research, priests of different orders are co-operating very well. They don't have to create a new religious order for the work they are doing, even though they are performing a type of work which is new in the Church. The same thing must have happened among women religious.

We are coming in the Church to many new forms of collective work, and we must be ready to respond to the Church's needs in the modern world. This will involve, especially at first, many problems of organization and re-organization. It will bring tensions to the Sisters in making these changes and in adapting their community life to the new functions.

Adaptation may mean not only changes in the organization of community life but also the possibility, at least for a time and for some places, of a *plural* type of religious life in convents and religious communities. We already have that in universities where Sisters of different congregations are living together while taking courses.

This, of course, brings us to the question of adaptation in spiritual exercises. Every congregation is very fixed with regard to its exercises, its choir, prayerbooks, and so on. We may have to come to greater unity as to these things. It is a very relative matter, the recital of this or that prayer every morning; we must realize that its importance is not absolute. I don't say that we have to lose the richness of the many spiritual currents in the Church, but that we should come to some kind of unification so that congregations could live together and not have each Sister saying her prayers in her own corner.

We shall probably also have to come to greater unity among many congregations; and with very small ones this may mean actually merging. This seems to be quite difficult, even if the congregations have the same origin and the same kind of spirituality. There are congregations with as few as twenty-five members who refuse to merge with any other. Of course this is really pathetic, and there is nothing to be done about it except to allow them to die out.

But this whole process of adaptation must take place, or at least begin to take place, within the next few years. Only congregations able to do this will survive. Only those congregations able to fulfill the new requirements—to face with courage the possibility of taking on new roles according to the needs of the universal Church and of each particular country, and to meet the problems of adaptation within the congregation itself, such as amending the constitutions or merging—will in the long run be able to survive.

And only those congregations which respond to the new needs of the Church will appear before the Church and the world as performing a real task in the Church, of giving a living testimony of love, of true charity in the world.

8 *The New Thought*

We come, then, to our final consideration as to the role of the Church in technical civilization: *the new thought.* We have spoken so often of the need for adaptation that we may have given the impression that nothing at all has been done. This is not true, because already we are in the process of an extraordinary number of evolutions, even in the field of theological thought.

ECCLESIOLOGY

All our thinking about ecclesiology is changing with the rediscovery of the universal, the collective, responsibility of the bishops of the world. Of course this involves a doctrine never lost sight of in the Church, one we shall always hold, but we are seeing it afresh because of the demands of our present-day world. A rediscovery, a re-examination, is taking place in ecclesiological theology. Not only with regard to the organization and collectivity of the bishops but with regard to the whole Church, her missionary activity, and the responsibility for mission countries.

We had come to such misconceptions about the missions that we saw them only as the Pope's responsibility, and therefore specialized congregations and orders for missionary activities were created. The bishops and priests in the dioceses for the most part felt and took little responsibility for the missions beyond collecting money or postage stamps.

Now we are becoming more and more aware of the truth that each bishop shares in the responsibility for the universal Church. Many bishops are taking these responsibilities seriously, sending priests to mission countries, asking through their dioceses for communities of Sisters to be sent to mission countries, or supporting groups of lay volunteers, such as PAVLA, to work in Latin America. This is causing a whole new outlook in the Church, many new activities, and a complete rethinking of the theology of the missions. Much of this new thought appears in Father Yves Congar's book on episcopal collegiality.

THE THEOLOGY OF TEMPORAL REALITIES

Our vision of the world, our theology of *temporal reality*, must be adapted to the world in development. It is a very different thing to live in a world full of blind, uncontrollable natural forces, a world where you are dependent upon nature and helpless before its whims, where you must suffer without understanding or relief, and your only defense is spiritual consolation and/or the use of some kind of magic against the forces over which you have no control. This is the world that was.

We are now in a world where nature has become for man an instrument for his progress, where the secrets of nature are being revealed daily, and those which remain hidden today give promise of future discovery. Man's whole attitude toward nature has changed—from a burden to be borne to a conquest to be effected.

And our theology of the world must take this change into account. We must come from a "spirituality of underdevelopment" to an awareness of our collective responsibilities in the temporal order.

MORAL THEOLOGY

The same thing is true of our *moral* theology. New discoveries in the world have given new dimensions to moral problems such as those of birth control, psychological and emotional disorders, nuclear war, civil rights, and so on. Not nearly enough progress has been made in our approach to these problems.

But some steps have been taken. Cardinal Suenens, in 1958, called together a group of Catholic biologists, theologians, and doctors to discuss and reflect upon some of these new problems and to keep up with the fresh discoveries. This group still meets regularly. Not long ago a meeting was organized with Protestant leaders and leaders of the Population Council to discuss birth control and population questions with the end in mind of reaching an understanding of one another's points of view.

Moral theology is faced with many other problems that have been brought to our attention in great part by psychology, and especially psychoanalysis. There is a profound renewal taking place in moral theology, and a new approach is being adopted which represents a movement from a logical, juridical attitude toward one based on the law of charity. But here again we are very slow in producing enough people adequately formed in these areas, capable of orienting our people and making the necessary theological judgments.

THE THEOLOGY OF PASTORAL WORK

The pastoral work of the Church must reflect the concern of the Church with all the aspects of our life in a changing world. Because we are living in a state of perpetual mutation we are faced with all kinds of new problems.

We are in an age when the Church will be faced always with new relationships in the world, with the necessity for new organizations, for new types of action, for new roles. This means also the need for a theological approach to the people of God which proceeds from an informed reflection upon existent realities, and an awareness that unchanging principles must always be applied in a changing world.

Index